Rome

Ancient Rome
Roman History and The Roman Empire

3rd Edition

By Roy Jackson

Table of Contents

Introduction

Chapter 1: Rome And Its Origin

Chapter 2: Romulus's Rule of Rome and His End

Chapter 3: The Roman Republic – Rise And Fall

Chapter 4: Julius Caesar

Chapter 5: The Era of The Emperors

Chapter 6: Disintegration Of The Roman Empire

Conclusion

© Copyright 2015 - All rights reserved.

In no way is it legal to reproduce, duplicate, or transmit any part of this document in either electronic means or in printed format. Recording of this publication is strictly prohibited and any storage of this document is not allowed unless with written permission from the publisher. All rights reserved.

The information provided herein is stated to be truthful and consistent, in that any liability, in terms of inattention or otherwise, by any usage or abuse of any policies, processes, or directions contained within is the solitary and utter responsibility of the recipient reader. Under no circumstances will any legal responsibility or blame be held against the publisher for any reparation, damages, or monetary loss due to the information herein, either directly or indirectly.

Respective authors own all copyrights not held by the publisher.

Legal Notice:

This book is copyright protected. This is only for personal use. You cannot amend, distribute, sell, use, quote or paraphrase any part or the content within this book without the consent of the author or copyright owner. Legal action will be pursued if this is breached.

Disclaimer Notice:

Please note the information contained within this document is for educational and entertainment purposes only. Every attempt has been made to provide accurate, up to date and reliable complete information. No warranties of any kind are expressed or implied. Readers acknowledge that the author is not engaging in the rendering of legal, financial, medical or professional advice.

By reading this document, the reader agrees that under no circumstances are we responsible for any losses, direct or indirect, which are incurred as a result of the use of information contained within this document, including, but not limited to, —errors, omissions, or inaccuracies.

Introduction

What is the recipe for a successful and long lasting Empire? Is it the number of provinces under its control? Or is it the number of victories garnered by the Empire in war? Or is it a stable constitution that holds the entire empire together? Or is it just the able leadership of great emperors?

Well, the answer is an ideal combination of all the four aforesaid components. Even if one of these factors is not taken into consideration, the survival of the Empire becomes a question. That was precisely the case when it came to the Roman Empire. History stands testimony to the many victories of Rome and its systematic expansion across the globe. But what went wrong despite all the victories?

Ancient Rome was the hearth for several young leaders like Julius Caesar and several artists and architects. Literature never flourished in the same fashion as it did under the Ancient Roman era. The Roman Empire stretched along the Mediterranean Sea, covering over 2.5 million square miles, and containing roughly around twenty percent of the world's entire population. Without a doubt, it was one of the largest and greatest empires of the ancient world. The effective strategies and ploys employed by the Roman army was an example worthy of being followed by all aspiring soldiers across the world. Ancient Roman society was a civilization that was highly developed for its time; in fact, its system of governance – *res publica* – served as an inspiration for modern day republics like those of France and the United States.

And yet, like any other kingdom or civilization, Rome fell. How did such a strong city suddenly disintegrate into nothingness?

If your curiosity to understand what made Rome a glorious empire and what resulted in its downfall, then you have found the right book! This book contains all that you need to know about Ancient Rome, starting from its discovery till its disintegration. In the first chapter of this book, I give an overview of how the city came into existence. In the second chapter, I explain the growth establishment of the Roman Republic, followed by a chapter on its growth. After this, I give you an exclusive chapter on Julius Caesar, after which I bring to you the details of the various emperors who took over the mantle of leadership in Rome following Caesar's death. And in the final chapter, I have dealt with the disintegration of the Empire.

I hope you find it an engaging and exciting journey!

Chapter 1: Rome And Its Origin

When it comes to the formation of a city, records are sketchy at best. And when we speak of an ancient city like Rome, which was born eons before modern civilization, it becomes very difficult to pin point a specific date when the city came into being. Myth and legend blend in with history, creating a story where the lines between fact and fiction blur. Archeology *does* help a little in separating the two, but more often than not, what we do know about the founding of Rome comes from the stories passed down in the oral tradition by the Ancient Romans themselves.

Rome's foundation myth is a fascinating tale that traces its roots all the way to the Trojan War. We all must have heard the proverb – *"Rome was not built in a day"*. Have we ever actually done the research to analyze how this infamous city came into existence? I guess not. But that is about to change now. In this chapter, I give to you the history of how Rome came into existence. By the end of this chapter, you sure would understand the rationale behind the aforesaid proverb.

Much of the following story is the tale told by an ancient Roman poet known as Virgil – in his most famous work, *Aeneid*, he outlines the tale of Aeneas, a fallen Trojan who flees the battlefield and ventures to Italy where he becomes the father of the Romans.

Trojan Ancestor – Aeneas and His Journey

The tale begins with the end of the Trojan War. With Paris defeated and Helen returned to her previous husband, Menelaus, and the city of Troy lying in ruins, the survivors banded together under the leadership if Aeneas. He rallied the fallen people and led them through the building of a fleet of ships, soon after which they departed the destroyed city. They traveled west, along the Mediterranean Sea, where they underwent many adventures – from being shipwrecked on the Cyclops, Polyphemus's island, to stopping at a newly founded Carthage under the rule of Queen Dido; they faced chaos, one after another, until they finally arrived in Italy.

And the conflicts did not end there. When Aeneas and his crew landed on the coast on Lavinium, the princess of the realm, Lavinia, was engaged to a man named Turnus. Aeneas courted Lavinia and she accepted him – but things would not be so easy for the lovers. Juno – who would later be one of the patron goddesses of Rome, and is the Roman equivalent of the Greek goddess, Hera – began to stir up trouble. She persuaded Lavinia's mother to demand that the princess be married only to Turnus, who was a ruler of the local people. And though Aeneas tried his best to prevent it, a war broke out, with Turnus leading an army against Aeneas and his forces.

After a long and hard battle, Aeneas defeated Turnus. By winning the war, not only did Aeneas keep Lavinia's hand in marriage, he also managed to win his own people the right to assimilate with the locals and become part of the natural landscape.

Virgil's *Aeneid* ends there, with the defeat of Turnus and the establishment of Aeneas in what would later become the Roman Empire. Fast forward to four score years later – legend believes that Rome was founded four hundred and thirty eight years after the fall of the Trojan empire. The younger son of Aeneas, Ascanius – also known as Iulus – went on to found Alba Longa, after the fall of his father. His descendants ruled the city after his death, one of which was Rhea Silvia – the mother of Remus and Romulus, who would found Rome, thus establishing the chronological connection between the Trojans and the Romans.

Romulus and Remus

The twin brothers, Remus and Romulus, founded Rome. Before we get to the twins, let me tell what happened to their mother. Close to four centuries after Alba Longa was established, Rhea Silvia was born to Numitor, who was took the throne after his father, Procas died. However, Numitor's younger brother, Amulius was greedy for power. The lure of the throne led him to assassinate not only Numitor's son, but also his own sons, so that no one would usurp him when he became king. Unfortunately for him, he was only partially successful. When he took the throne, a prophecy was said to have been made, predicting that the offspring of Rhea Silvia would overthrow him and restore the empire to Numitor.

Obviously, this enraged him and he did everything he could to prevent such a thing from coming to pass – he made Rhea Silvia a *Vestal Virgin*. Vestal Virgins were priestesses to *Vesta*, the goddess of the hearth (the Roman equivalent of the Greek Goddess Hestia). These women were sworn to celibacy and they cultivated a sacred fire that was not allowed to go out. Their chastity was their greatest honor, and in making Rhea Silvia a Vestal Virgin, Amulius was confident that he had managed to stop the foretelling of his end from coming true.

But the gods themselves were invested in the founding of Rome – or so it seemed. Legend tells us that Rhea Silvia, as she was walking through the forest, came upon none other than Mars himself – the god of war (Roman equivalent of Greek God Aries), with whom she spent the night. Accounts vary – some tell us that she was raped by the god, while others state that she simply lay with an unknown man whom she later proclaimed to be Mars to ward social stigma off her offspring. In any case, most people accept that it was Mars who lay with Rhea Silvia, and it was he who fathered two sons on her – Remus and Romulus.

But theirs was not the happiest of tales. When Amulius learnt of Rhea Silvia's twin children, he ordered for her to be imprisoned and buried alive, and commanded a servant to kill the boys. As is so often the case, the servant was unable to murder such innocent life, and in a fit of mercy, set them adrift in a basket on the river Tiber. The water took them to the banks of a pool, where a she-wolf – called *lupa* – found them. She had just lost her own cubs, and ended up suckling the hungry boys with her milk. Myth even tells us that the boys were guarded by the river-god Tibernius, who pushed them gently towards the bank and gave them to the *lupa* to suckle. A woodpecker – *Picus* – fed them.

Legends following this particular scene are murky and confused. One tale follows the boys as they are then found by Fastulus and his wife Acca Larentia, who raised them as their own, in the life of shepherds. The most popularly told version, however, is that of Remus and Romulus being raised by the she-wolf herself, before coming into their destiny to overthrow Amulius.

Interestingly, another Roman tradition has Acca Larentia cast in the role of a sacred prostitute, and one of the Roman slang for prostitute was the word *lupa*.

Meanwhile, as the boys were growing up, Rhea Silvia, imprisoned, was ordered to be killed. She was then rescued by the same river-god of the Tiber, Tiberinus, who took her to be his bride.

Discovery of Rome

Every version of the founding myth of Rome tells of the boys growing up as shepherds. Destiny came calling, however, when once they came into conflict with some of Amulius's shepherds. Remus was captured, legend tells us and then taken to Amulius. It did not take the usurper long to identify his great-nephew, and to order him killed. To save his brother, Romulus stirred up a rebellion and with a band of shepherds behind him, fought against Amulius and had him killed, liberating Numitor. The boys were offered the throne co-jointly, but they refused, choosing instead, to restore their grandfather to power. They decided then to leave Alba Longa and found their own city.

And that was when their troubles began. Neither Remus nor Romulus could agree to the location of where they would establish their new home. The ancient city of Rome was built in and around seven hills – Caelian Hill, Aventine Hill, Esquiline Hill, Palatine Hill, Capitoline Hill, Viminal Hill and the Quirinal Hill. Before the city itself was constructed, however, Remus and Romulus had to decide where they wanted to start building it – the former wanted to build upon Aventine, and the latter wanted the city set around Palatine Hill.

They twin brothers argued for a long time before finally agreeing to pray to the gods to solve their problem, by the practice of augury. In simple terms, augury was the ancient Roman way of interpreting omens by observing birds in flight, depending upon which a situation or circumstance could be auspicious or inauspicious – either favorable or unfavorable. The brothers hoped that this would solve their conflict without too much difficulty.

And so, they took up their respective positions on their favored hills – Remus set up a sacred space on Aventine Hill while Romulus did the same on the Palatine Hill and both waited for the signs from the gods. In the end, Remus saw only six auspicious birds

– Romulus, on the other hand, had seen twelve, and claimed himself the winner. Remus opposed him, advocating that he had seen all six of his birds *first*, and the two continued to fight, before Romulus finally dug a trench – some versions of the myth say he built a wall – around Palatine Hill to demarcate the boundaries of his city.

What happened after that is, once again, a very confused and blurred tale that has many versions. Some say that Remus, unhappy with the whole situation, criticized the city his brother was building. He leapt over the wall in an attempt to belittle Romulus, who, enraged by his brother, killed him with the words, *"So perish every one that shall hereafter leap over my wall."* Another account tells of how Remus was killed by a blow to the head with a spade that was wielded by Fabius, who served as Romulus's commander. And still others say that Romulus deeply regretted his brother's death and so had him buried with all ceremony and honor.

No matter the tale, all accounts agree on the same thing – the foundation of the city caused a tiff between the brothers that led to the end of Remus, with Romulus setting up as the new ruler of the city he founded. Thus, in what is accepted today to be 753 BC, Romulus established the ancient Roman Empire, and named the city after himself – *Roma*.

Chapter 2: Romulus's Rule of Rome and His End

Soon after setting himself up as the ruler of Rome, Romulus established the city's government, which would pave the way for a Republic much later. He divided his men into cavalry and infantry, and from the general populace, he handpicked a hundred men to be his council. These were men of noble rank, who were wealthy and powerful. Romulus dubbed them *Patricians* – they were to be the fathers of Rome, and protect it as they would their own children. With them, he formed the Senators, who would advise him and have an important say in the matters of governance.

Slowly, the city began to expand to include refugees, runaways, exiles and the like. Five of the seven hills that the later Roman city would rest on were brought into play at this time, as the city began to open its boundaries to make space for the newer citizens who were pouring in. but there was a huge problem – there was a distinct lack of the female populace, which meant there were not enough marriageable women.

To resolve the issue, Romulus invited the Sabines and Latins, who were their neighbors, to a festival conducted at the *Circus Maximus*, which served as Ancient Rome's chariot racing stadium, located between the valley of the Aventine and the Palatine Hills. The festival was to be organized in honor of the god, *Consus*, who was the ancient Roman patron and protector of grains. Some versions of the tale also cite the festival celebrated in honor of *Neptune*, whose realm was the sea.

With the Sabines and Latins came their womenfolk. Romulus and his men organized fun games and kept the male population of their visitors plied with wine constantly, so that it was not long before they were drunk and distracted. It did not take them too long to spirit the daughters away after that, and take them into the heart of the city, where the Romans began their attempts to convince them to stay and marry and raise families with them. Most of them were eventually persuaded.

Of course, the Sabine and Latin men were hardly going to let such a deed go unanswered. The Latin towns of Caenina, Antemnae and Crustumerium marched into Rome, demanding the return of their daughters, but were soundly defeated by Romulus and his men. Their defeat also meant more territory for Rome. The land was seized and added to the Roman Empire, but Romulus was a magnanimous ruler – he did not enslave any of his new citizens, simply making them a part of his landscape.

The conflict with the Sabines was a little bit more complicated. Their king, Titus Tatius, marched straight into the Capitololine citadel, where the citadel commander's daughter, Tarpeia, let them in. She was promised the golden bracelets on their arms for doing so; however, as soon as they entered, they crushed her to death with their shields. The Sabines then met the Romans in an open battle at the *comitium,* which was the open-air public meeting space where later on, political and judicial assembly would take place. The Romans retreated under the attack, sequestering themselves within the Palatine Hill, wherein they called upon the god Jupiter for help. Soon after, they managed to fight the Sabines off and drove their armies to the point where the senate house, *Curia Hostilia* would later stand.

At this point, having had enough of the war, thirty of the captured Sabine women themselves intervened between the two peoples. They begged for unity amongst the Sabines and the Romans, and finally, a truce was declared between the two warring armies. The Romans made Palatine their home, while the Sabines based themselves on the Quirinal and both Romulus and Titus Tatius took up the mantle of rulers, establishing themselves as co-regents of the kingdom. The *Comitium* served as the common centre of government and culture for their joined borders, and another hundred Sabine elders joined the Patricians as part of the Roman Senate.

There was a definite cultural exchange as the two races mingled. The Sabines, for instance, took to the Roman calendar, and the Romans, in exchange adopted the usage of the Sabine armor and oblong shields in battle. For five years, the empire flourished under the joint rule of Romulus and Tatius, who even expanded their borders further by defeating the Alban colony of the *Camerini*. But the end of the partnership was nigh upon them; Tatius sheltered within their halls some allies who had plundered the Lavinians, to whom Romulus was related through his mother's side. To protect the refugees, Tatius murdered the ambassadors who were sent from Lavinium to extract justice on the criminals. Angered by his actions, Romulus – backed up by the Roman Senate – demanded that Tatius go to Lavinium and offer an apology to appease them. Reluctantly, Tatius agreed and left – he did not return. He was assassinated in Lavinium, leaving Romulus the sole ruler of Rome.

The rule of Romulus was long; he set up an administrative system that inspires people even today. He organized them according to tribe, each of which elected a tribune of members to represent them in civil, military and religious matters. In many ways, the tribunes became a small district government of their own – they performed sacrifices on behalf of their people, commanded levies during times of war and represented their own in the State.

Romulus then went on to divide each tribe into smaller factions known as the *curiae* of ten each – these were assembly councils where official decisions were discussed and made. Thus, at the end, there were thirty *curiae* that constituted the *Comitia Curiata* or the *Curiate Assembly*. Any proposals for policy changes by Romulus and/or the senate would have to be offered to the Curiate Assembly for acceptance, which would then vote on it. In this manner, despite Rome being a monarchy, Romulus introduced a republican air to the idea of governance.

He went on to form a personal guard called the *Celeres*, which was comprised of three hundred of Rome's best horsemen. Some believe that these guards were named after Romulus's second-in-command, Celer, who, in one version of the founding myth, was the one who killed Romulus's twin, Remus. Either way, Celer was the second most powerful authority within the State, and in Romulus's absence, had command of the armies and the government.

From then on, Rome only grew in its size. Romulus waged wars to expand his territory endlessly. The first to go were the *Fidenae*, who in a colossal mistake attacked Rome to seize provisions during a famine.

Romulus defeated them easily and established his territory there – only to be opposed by the *Etruscans of Veii,* who protested a Roman garrison at Fidenae. They wanted the town returned to its people, and Romulus refused, subduing them when they attacked Rome. In the end, they were forced to accept a hundred-year truce. Romulus's third victory came at the defeat of the *Crustumini,* who had murdered the Roman colonists sent to their territory. Romulus responded swiftly by destroying their armies and adding their land to his.

Romulus's grandfather, Numitor died not long after. The people of Alba Longa wanted him to take the throne, since he was the rightful blood heir. Romulus brought the city within his territory, and adapted their government to that of a Roman model, but did not rule them directly. He taught them to hold annual elections and pick one of their own to represent them as Roman governor in the Senate.

For all his democratic attitude outside, however, Romulus began to exhibit autocratic behavior within the walls of his own city. The Senate, set up initially to keep his power in check, lost its influence in the making of laws and administration – Romulus's word was edict and had to be followed to the letter. The Senate's resentment turned to hatred when he took to dividing the newly conquered territories among his soldiers without the consent of the Patricians.

And therein began the downfall of Romulus, founder of Rome. Legend has it that he disappeared mysteriously, in either a storm or a whirlwind, soon after he offered a public sacrifice at Quirinal Hill. Suspicion often falls on the Senate to have grown tired of his indifference to their power and have him spirited away. Many believe that they wanted to take the government into their own hands, and wanted to rid themselves of the only obstacle in their way.

To throw the accusations flung at them away, it is said that they raised Romulus to the role of a divinity. A man of immense popularity, Proculus was made to swear that he saw Romulus lifted up to heaven, in full armor, and heard the king call out that they should, henceforth, spread his name forth as Quirinus, a divine entity of Rome. Whether this was part of the Senate's plan or whether Romulus truly disappeared into the heavens – the truth is unclear. All we do know is that Romulus vanished, and as a result, catapulted to the status of a divine being, whose last edict was to command his people to choose a new king. Debate sprung up immediately – should the new king be Roman or Sabine? The argument went on for a year, during which time, the members of the Senate exercised the royal power in rotation, for five days in a row each. Finally, Numa Pompilius, of Sabine origin was elected to be the next king of Rome's rulers. He became the legendary second king, succeeding Romulus.

Roman Kingdom

Ancient Rome started as a monarchy under the leadership of Romulus, its founder. There aren't many records that exist of the ancient Roman Kingdom and hence little is certain about its history. However, it is asserted that the Roman Kingdom began around the river Tiber in Italy with settlements slowly flourishing around for miles. The Roman Kingdom was successful mainly due to its strategic location around the Palatine Hill, which provided an easily defendable position. The early history of ancient Rome suggests that it was ruled by seven kings before the monarchy was overthrown and democracy was established. The reason why there aren't many records related to ancient Rome is that the Gauls destroyed almost all of Rome's historical records when they ransacked the city. The Roman Kingdom was based on a vast set of principles and guidelines that dictated how the kingdom was to be run and divided the powers among the officials.

The Constitution

The Constitution of the Roman Kingdom was a set of rules and guidelines that did not have a physical presence; it originated through precedent. The Constitution was controlled solely by the king who had the final authority in all matters. His powers included appointing officials, delegating powers and establishing laws.

The king did not take the decisions related to the state alone; he was advised by the Roman Senate that was lead only by the aristocracy. The Roman Kingdom was a monarchy in all matters, the king was free to do as he wishes, and he wasn't obligated to take any advice from the Senate. Further, there was the 'Curiate Assembly' that the king could refer to if he was in need of a vote on a certain matter, but he was free to ignore their decisions as well.

Rome was a religious country centered on a Pope, who was supposed to be the vessel of God. Although, the Pope did not exercise any power in political matters, the king was obligated to a certain extent to listen to his opinion. For this purpose, a popular assembly was set up as a way for the Pope as well the People of Rome to express their notions. The major function of this assembly was to give the People of Rome a platform to be heard, the organizational structure was based on people's curiae. The popular assembly served other functions as well, such as a trial court for state matters and a podium for public announcements.

Executive Magistrates

The officials that were elected by popular vote in ancient Rome were known as Executive Magistrates of the Roman Kingdom. The Roman king was the principle executive magistrate and all the others were his subordinate. The king was the most powerful man in all of Rome and he exercised absolute power. He was the commander in chief of the Roman army, chief priest, chief executive, chief judge and chief lawyer. He had the right to appoint all officials and determine their powers.

The king had absolute power, but that did not mean that there were no laws or precedents that overlooked his ruling of the state. His powers were regulated through a statutory organization known as the 'Imperium' (Command in Latin).

The king wasn't bestowed with power on appointment, but rather he gained his power through democratic elections and similarly, could be thrown from his office. Thus, the king's relatives did not succeed him in office and a new king was appointed through popular vote. He also did not receive any divine recognition, which was reserved for the Pope. After the death of the king, the ruling power passed to the Roman Senate for an interim period, the Senate selected an Interrex to carry out the election for a new king. The king was then elected through a democratic vote by the People of Rome, the Roman Senate granted him his powers and he was anointed by the Imperium.

Roman Kings

Rome was founded around 753 BC by its first king Romulus, who was also the first executive magistrate. He created the principles and guidelines on which the Roman Kingdom functioned. Rome had seven legendary kings that ruled for over 2000 years before the monarchy was overthrown. All historical records of ancient Rome were destroyed after the city was ransacked because of which there isn't any accurate information about the kings of ancient Rome.

Chief Executive

The king was granted Imperium by the senate through which he had supreme control over the military, judiciary and executives. The Imperium of the king was his most powerful tool and prevented him from ever being prosecuted for any crime. The king was the only person in all of Rome that was granted the Imperium, which is why he exercised absolute control over all matters of Rome and hence was the commander-in-chief of the Roman military.

There wasn't any law that protected the citizens from the misuse of the Imperium during this period, which is why the king could further use it to exercise control over citizens.

Since the king had absolute power, he also had the right to appoint all the officials that served Rome. The king handpicked the tribunus celerum who served as both the commander of the Celeres, the king's personal guard and the tribune of the roman tribe Ramnes. The tribune accompanied the king's ascend to the throne and left his position with the death of the king. The tribune itself exercised a lot of power, but was subordinate to the king in all aspects, it had the power to convene the Curiate Assembly and put legislations in front of it.

Other officers appointed directly by the king include, praefectus urbi, who was the warden of Rome. The praefectus took over the king's position in his absence, which meant that he exercised all of the king's power and even held the Imperium in his stead. The king also had the power to appoint people in the Senate.

Chief Priest

After his appointment, the king was considered to be the chief augur and he alone could perform auspices to know the will of the gods. Rome was a God fearing nation, which is why no public business took place without consulting the gods through auspices. The king was supposed to be the vessel of God to guide Rome and hence he was viewed as the arbitrator between the People of Rome and God. This is why the king was viewed as a holy spirit with divine notions. The king exercised all power over the religious ceremonies of the nation, he even had control over the calendar and set up dates for rituals, he even appointed religious officers at the lower levels. Romulus was famous as an augur, as he was said to be blessed by the gods for finding Rome. The second king Nuna Pompilius started the order of Pontiffs and through them he laid the foundations of religious principles.

Chief Legislator

The Senate and Curiate assembly were the judicial and executive authorities, but did not possess any power under the king, they were not independent and could not take any decisions without the will of the king. They couldn't even hold an assembly by their own choice and discuss important matters unless the king called for them and ordered them to discuss affairs of the state. The Senate was subordinate even to the Curiate assembly in terms of holding power, the assembly could pass the laws that were agreed upon by the king, but the Senate did not hold any power and was an institution set up to honor the aristocrats. It was essentially a body to advise the king in matters of state, but did not have any power over the actions that were to be taken for the prosperity of Rome. It was the king's choice to pay attention to them or not to. The only exception to the king's power was that he could not declare war against another nation without the approval of the Senate and Curiate assembly.

Chief Judge

The king's Imperium gave him absolute power over not only military related matters, but also appointed him as the legal prosecutor for all kinds of judgments based on Roman law. He was the legal advisor and chief justice of Rome. Since the king could not attend to every case himself, he appointed pontiffs at the lower level to pass judgment in his name but even then he had the power to rule over a pontiff's judgment. Therefore, he was the highest authority in all criminal and civil cases. If the Curiate assembly agreed, then they could appeal to a king's decision and have him formally review the case again.

There was a small council that was set up to advice the king during the trials, but this council was only an advisory body and did not have any control over the king's decision. There were other officials who were appointed by the king to help him investigate the cases such as two criminal detectives and he also had a two-man criminal court.

Election of the Kings

After the death of the king, the power of the king passed on to the Senate and Rome entered a period of Interregnum. The senate was responsible to take decisions regarding matters related to the state and it also had the responsibility to appoint a new king. The Senate would gather and collectively appoint an interrex to serve as the king for five days, during which he had to conduct democratic elections for the appointment of a new king, this was the only power the interrex had and could not exercise any other power bestowed upon the king. If the elections could not be conducted within these five days, then the interrex would appoint another senator as the new interrex for a period of five days. This process was continued on rotation basis till a new king was appointed. If an interrex finally decided on a nominee for kingship, then he would bring forth this nominee in front of the senate who would formally review him. The process only moved to the Curiate Assembly if the Senate approved a nominee, the interrex took over the proceedings as the election of the king was carried out in the Curiate Assembly.

The nominee for kingship was presented in front of the Curiate Assembly; hence the people of Rome could either accept their king or reject him by voting. If the nominee was accepted as king, then he did not enter office immediately, but had to wait for two more important acts to be carried out.

Firstly, it was important to consult the augur to know the will of the gods through an auspice. If the omens were favorable that would mean that the gods accept the nominee as the high priest and king of Rome. The ceremony that took place was carried out by an augur who placed the nominee on a citadel made of stone as the people of Rome watched. The augur would read the signs and announce whether the gods were in favor of the nominee or not, thus confirming that the king was a divine soul fit to be a mediator between the people of Rome and the gods.

Secondly, the Imperium had to be bestowed upon the king to anoint him with powers worthy of a king. The previous act only appointed someone as the king, but did not give him the powers to rule over Rome. So, the king himself had to put forth a law in front of the Curiate assembly to grant him Imperium, the assembly would pass this law and finally declare the person as king of the Roman Kingdom.

Although, it is said that these elections were democratic as the people selected their leader, many disagree because the first part of the process was carried out by the Senate. This is why many believe that it was the Senate, which had absolute control and influence when it came appointing a new king of Rome.

Kings of Rome

Numa Pompillus

Numa Pompillus was the second king of the Roman Kingdom and he succeeded the founder and first king of Rome, Romulus. He wasn't originally from Rome, but from the Sabine region that joined Rome after its conquest. He was an influential political figure; there are many important political and religious institutions that are dedicated to him.

Numa was the youngest son of Pomponius and it is said that he was born on the day of Rome's founding. Numa lived without any luxuries for his whole life and dedicated his life towards discipline. Numa was married to Tatia, the only daughter of the Sabine king, Titus Tatius. Numa left the Sabine region and lived in the Roman countryside after the death of his beloved wife Tatia. This is where he resided for many years before he was appointed as the king of Rome.

Numa had one daughter and five sons from both his marriages. He had a daughter named Pompilia with his first wife, Tatia and five sons with his second wife,

Lucretia called Pompo, Pinus, Calpus, Mamercus and Numa.

Following the constitution of the Roman Kingdom, after Romulus's death, the Senate exercised all power with each member having 5 days to rule in rotation, this period was known as Interregnum. There was a quarrel between the Romans and the Sabines on the appointment of a king, after a lot of debate, the Sabine Numa Pompillus was elected as the king.

Numa was very cunning and did not want anyone to challenge his rise to power, which is why he refused to accept the position at first. His father, the Sabine king and his sons tried to persuade him to accept the offer but he refused. He later agreed to a meeting with the Senate and was greeted with enthusiasm by the People of Rome. He agreed to be the king only if the augur asked the gods for approval. The augur carried out a ritual and consulted Jupiter; the omens were in favor of his appointment. Hence, Numa accepted the offer of kingship.

Numa's first order as the king was to discontinue the "Celeres" a band of 100 soldiers that were appointed as the personal guard for the king. Everyone saw this as a gesture of humility.

Numa was also said to be an agent of god due to his many relations and connections with various gods and goddesses. He was celebrated throughout Rome for his piety and wisdom, he was favorably accepted by Jupiter as the king of Rome and it is said that he had connections with other deities as well. His connection with the nymph Egeria is very famous, it is said that she taught him the arts of being a good legislator. Every night Numa would visit the nymph and she would teach him how to observe important rituals for the prosperity of Rome and its people. He abided by all the laws and superstitions to act as a role model for the citizens and gain their favor. It is also said that he consulted the two minor gods, Picus and Faunus to deliver prophecies relating to the events of the future.

He respected the great teachings that he had been given all his life by the nymph Egeria and the Muses. He recorded all of his divine teachings and thoughts in various books, and instructed that these books be buried with him. He never taught his philosophies to anyone because he did not believe in verbal knowledge that could not be preserved. These books covered a variety of subjects; half of the books were focused on the priesthoods he had established, mainly Pontifices, Salii, Famines and Fetiales and the other books covered teachings he had been given and his philosophies. These books were buried with him as instructed by him to the Senate. Years later, his tomb was revealed due to a natural calamity and the books were found preserved in perfect condition. The books were reviewed by the Senate, who ruled that they were inappropriate for public knowledge and had them burned.

Numa tried to please Jupiter by inviting him to a battle of wits in order to gain a ritual of protection against lightning and thunder. At this time, a baneful disease had spread throughout Rome killing majority of the population. Reportedly, a shield flew out of the sky and came to Numa, who declared it as an omen of protection from Jupiter himself. After this incident, the plague slowly receded. Numa understood the importance of the shield and how it was a divine connection between Rome and its gods. Therefore, he ordered the creation of eleven shields that were completely identical to the first one, so that even Numa couldn't tell which one was the original. These shields were called the ancillia, that is, shields dedicated to Jupiter; they were carried by the Salli priests every year in various rallies.

Numa was a god-fearing man whose dedication towards the divine powers helped Rome through many difficulties. One of his first acts after being appointed as King was to construct a temple for Janus, the god of doors and choices. The temple indicated the two choices of peace and war. The doors of the temple were always shut during the reign of Numa; the doors were shut after peace was achieved with Rome's neighbors.

Numa also started the cult of Terminus, the god of boundaries. It involved various rituals at the boundaries, thresholds and lines to teach Romans the importance of respecting other's property and keeping non-violent relations with their neighbors. The cult of terminus preached non-violence and the absence of murder.

Numa's major contribution in terms of reforms was the introduction of a new calendar format, which adjusted the solar and lunar years thus creating the months of January and February.

Numa was a well loved king and lead Rome to prosperity; he finally died in 673 BC due to old age and was succeeded by Tullus Hostillius.

Tullus Hostillius

Tullus Hostillius was the third king of the Roman Kingdom, his predecessor was Numa Pompillus and his successor was Ancus Marcius. He ruled for about 30 years and was said to be the most war-favoring king of ancient Rome.

He was of Sabine origin and his grandfather was Hostus Hostillius who had fought Romulus himself during the war between Rome and Sabine. He is most famous for his defeat of Alba Longa in a war that lasted over 10 years. Alba Longa was a neighboring city that had caused many problems for Rome such as disruptions in travelling and import of supplies. Alba Longa was finally defeated by a fight between three roman champions and three Albans. It soon became a vassal state of Rome and supplied many food products for its people. Rome was betrayed by the Alban dictator, Mettius Fufetius who sought to destroy Rome from inside. Tullus was enraged by this and ordered the destruction of Alba Longa and forced all the Albans to migrate to Rome, where they were given the status of Roman citizens. He also waged successful war against Fidenae, Veii and the Sabines.

Rome was a religious nation whose king was said to be the mediator between the gods and the people of Rome. Tullus wasn't a very successful king because he did not give much importance to religious matters, since he deemed them to be unworthy of a king's attention. It was believed that due to his intolerance, Rome was struck with natural calamities at the end of his reign. It included a shower of stones on the Alban Mount, a loud voice complaining about the lack of devotion showed by the Romans and a bubonic plague struck in Rome. Tullus finally started believing in the superstitions when he fell gravely ill and read the books written by Nuna for the worship of Jupiter. However, Tullus wasn't a religious person and did not understand how to carry out the ceremony because of which he performed the wrong rituals and hence, enraged Jupiter who destroyed him and his house by lightning.

There isn't much known about the early life of Tullus except that he was raised by shepherds just like Romulus, his major achievements include expanding Rome by taking over neighboring territories and doubling its population.

Tullus also ordered the construction of the famous Senate house, the Curia Hostilia, whose remains can still be found in ancient Rome. The only logical evidence that suggests that the Senate was built by Tullus is its name, except that many historians have argued that the creation of the Senate house might have been after his reign. Some historians even argue that the Alba Longa may have been destroyed by some other nation instead of Rome. The reason for this lack of knowledge is that many of the historical records of Rome were destroyed when the city was ransacked by the Gauls, which has led to inaccuracy in historical facts.

Ancus Marcius

Ancus Marcius was the fourth king of the Roman kingdom, he was the son of Marcius, who was a close friend of the second king Nuna Pompilius and married Pomilia, daughter of Nuna Pompilius. After the death of Tullus Hostillius, the senate held the power to rule till a new king was appointed, this ended when an interrex was appointed who carried out democratic election for the appointment of a new king.

The first act of Ancus Marcius as king was to make sure that the religious rituals written by Nuna Pompilius were preserved forever. He ordered the Pontifex Maximus to copy the sacred text and had it displayed to the public. This was done to make sure that all the rites and rituals were performed properly.

He waged war against a small band of villages situated near Rome known as the Latins. The reason for the war was trespassing by the villagers into the Roman territory, specifically the Aventine Hill. The Latins were confident that Ancus would not wage war on them just like his grandfather Nuna, who was a peaceful king. Ancus did try a peaceful solution to the problem, by sending a delegating to talk with the Latins but received a threatening reply. Hence, the Romans waged war on the Latins, it's also historically important because this was the first time that they had declared war through the rites of the fetials.

He marched from Rome with a huge army to fight against the Latins; his first victory came at the tower of Politorium. He allowed the citizens that were situated here to settle on the Aventine Hill as Roman citizens. The Latins came back and settled in the town of Politorium, Ancus was enraged by this and proceeded to demolish the town so that no one would return to it. He continued his plight by taking over the villages of Tellenae and Ficana.

The deciding battle of the war took place in the town of Medullia. The town was the strongest base for the Latin army and was firmly fortified. The war took place outside the town and the Romans had an easy victory. The Romans found a lot of treasure in their conquest and returned home with vast booty. The Latin citizens were allowed to settle on the base of the Aventine Hill, by the temple of Murica. Ancus Marcius carried out many structural changes in the city; he added Janiculum to the city gave it protection by fortifying it with a wall and connected it to the city by a bridge across the Tiber. He was also responsible for the construction of the city's first ever prison, known as Mamertine Prison.

He was the first king to set up a Roman outpost at sea, by finding the port of Ostia. He used this port as a salt producing area and took the port of Silva Maesia and the coastal region around it. He ordered the building of many temples dedicated to Jupiter and Neptune.

Lucius Tarquinius Priscus

Lucius Tarquinius Priscus, also known as Tarquin the elder was the fifth king of the Roman Kingdom. He ruled for a period of 20-30 years and was married to Tanaquil.

Lucius came from the distant land of Etruria that was conquered by Rome. His name in the native language of Etruria translates to 'the king'. He inherited a huge fortune after his father's death, later he tried to make a career in politics. He could not enter any political office in Etruria because of his father's Greek origin and was very disappointed. He then shifted to Rome on his wife's suggestion, to try and start a political career there. It is said that he arrived in Rome on a chariot and as soon as he crossed the boundary an eagle took his cap, then circled around and dropped it on his head. Tanaquil had the skills of an oracle and took this as a great omen for future prosperity. Lucius was a very sweet and chivalrous person; this earned him a lot of respect in Rome. He was even noticed by the king who appointed him as guardian to his two sons.

Rome did not have hereditary monarchy, the king was appointed through popular vote among the Senate and the people. When Ancus Marcius died, Lucius convinced everyone to appoint him as king over Ancus's two sons. His argument was that the two were only children and could not lead Rome, while he was a talented bureaucrat who could handle this great responsibility.

Lucius brought many changes to Rome; he increased the capacity of the Senate by adding one hundred more members from leading minor families of Rome. He also waged war on the Latins and took the town of Apiolae from them; he brought back a huge booty back to Rome, from this town.

The Sabines also attacked Rome during his rule; they were backed by many other nations as well. Lucius raised the numbers of the Roman militia to include five thousand more men, which was a decisive factor in winning the war. The Sabines almost breached the boundaries of Rome, the war finally ended with bloody fighting on the streets just outside Rome. The Sabines had to agree to the peace accord that was given by Lucius, Rome got two towns from the Sabine territory known as Equites and Collatia. He appointed his nephew, Arruns Tarquinius as supreme commander of the military force there. He also brought many Latin cities under the rule of Rome such as Cameria, Ameriola, Medullia, Ficulea, Corniculum and Nomentum.

The wars against Rome did not end here, five Etruscan cities declared war against Rome and soon seven more Etruscan cities joined them to destroy Rome. The Etruscan started taking over Roman countryside and finally took over the Roman colony at Fidenae, from where the Etruscans waged war on Rome. After several years of fighting, Lucius again defeated the enemies of Rome and subjugated those who had taken part in the war.

Servius Tullius

Servius Tullius was the sixth and the last king of the Roman kingdom. He was the second king of Rome to have an Etruscan dynasty. He was the first king of Rome to be elected by popular support and not by election through the Senate. Hence, he was the first king of Rome to be elected without referring to the people.

Several sources point out that he was chosen by the gods to be the king of Rome, the son of an enslaved Latin princess, he was picked to be the king when a ring of fire was seen above his head right after his birth.

Servius was very popular among the masses, and the most successful king of Rome. He was an extraordinary military commander and had success in wars against the Veii and the Etruscans. He expanded the territory under Rome to include Quirinal, Esquiline and Viminal hills. He also started the tradition of the Compitalia festival, ordered the building of temples for Diana and Fortuna and brought into public use the first ever Roman coinage system. He was a kind man and helped the lower classes of Rome, even though the aristocrats advised him not to. He reigned for 44 years and it was the longest among all the kings till he was murdered by his own daughter and her husband. His son in law Tarquinius Superbus then took the throne, but was removed due to his arrogance. His death resulted in the end of the Roman Kingdom and start of the Roman Republic.

Servius's mother was Ocrisia, who was a Latin noblewoman living with her husband in the town of Corniculum. She was brought to Rome while she was pregnant and alone as her husband was killed at the battle of Corniculum. She was offered as a slave to Tanaquil, wife of the king, but she wasn't treated as a slave due to her status of a noblewoman. She gave birth to Servius while performing the domestic rites of the Vestal Virgin, while performing these rites; she gave birth to Silvius who appeared with a fire over his head. This was seen as an omen of the divine God Vulcan by Tanaquil. Hence, Servius was considered a divine soul who was destined for greatness by the gods themselves and even his mother's status as a slave could not alter his destiny. Tanaquil and Ocrisia did not reveal this incident to anyone else for the time being.

Since Servius was the son of a slave working under the royal family, in a way he became the extended family of Tarquin. He soon became Tarquin's adopted son when he married his daughter known as Gegania.

Before his appointment as the king of Rome, many people witnessed a fire above his head while he was sleeping, this was a divine sign and many believed that he was sent by the gods. He was very loyal to the king and an excellent son in law. He was acclaimed even in his early years as a great strategist and military commander.

Servius was appointed as the king a bit later after the death of his predecessor Lucius. Ancus, the earlier king had two sons who were two young to be considered for kingship and hence were not even nominated, while Servius being considered a divine soul was appointed by popularity both in the people of Rome and the Roman Senate. The sons still wanted power for themselves and hired assassins to kill him. The assassins failed to kill him, but fatally wounded his wife, Tarquinius. After this incident, Servius was accepted as the king by all of Rome. Although, his wife did not survive the attack and died of her wounds, her death was the reason for the appointment of Servius as king. The Senate elected him as king while the two sons of Ancus fled Rome to exiled lands beyond the Roman boundary.

In his early days as king, Servius gathered a great army to fight against Veii and Etruscans. He was a strong willed person and succeeded in destroying his enemies. This led to a great increase in his popularity. Servius was a lowborn person that is why he helped the commoners get more power by giving them voting rights.

Servius had two daughters, Tullia the younger and Tullia the elder. He married his daughters to the two sons of the previous king Lucius Tarquinius. The younger one married Arruns Tarquinius and the elder one married Lucius Tarquinius.

Chapter 3: The Roman Republic – Rise And Fall

Rome has gone from being a small kingdom, to a republic to an empire that extended its hegemony over the entire Mediterranean world. Every civilization has had its own history, its own pitfalls and glories. So was the case with the Roman civilization. Since its discovery, the city has had its own problems associated with its sustenance. In this chapter, let us look at how the city survived through the ages.

Fall of the Monarchy

Since its discovery in 753 B.C., Rome was held together purely because of the system of monarchy that was being practiced there. The monarch rulers didn't see that the end was nearing. With the birth of 509 B.C., the end of monarchy became certain. While historians are not quite sure of the truth of it, the Roman Kingdom was said to have had exactly seven kings, including Romulus. However, while they are unsure of the exact number of rulers that succeeded the founder of the city, they do agree that the last of them was Tarquin the Proud, who was overthrown by Lucius Junius Brutus. This incident was triggered by the rape of Lucretia, a noble woman who was respected by the citizens of Rome, by the son of Tarquin. This brought about the end of monarchy in Rome.

The story goes as such. To begin with, let me tell you the rise of Tarquin himself. His full name was Lucius Tarquinius Superbus, and he was either the son or the grandson of Lucius Tarquinius Priscus, the fifth king of Rome, and Tanaquil. Soon after the death of Ancus Marcius, Tanaquil engineered circumstances so that her husband would ascend to the throne, and when he was assassinated, she put Servius Tullius in her husband's place, ignoring her own sons.

Well aware of the domestic strife that was caused; Servius Tullius married his daughters – Tullia Major and Tullia Minor – to Lucius Tarquinius and his brother, Arruns, respectively. However, the marriages were not what they were expected to be; the elder Tullia was sweet and easygoing and ambitious Lucius Tarquinius found her tiresome. On the other hand, the younger Tullia, of a fierce temperament, came to despise the mild-mannered Arruns. Therein seemed the match of the heavens – the younger Tullia and Lucius Tarquinius teamed up to kill their siblings, following which they married each other.

Their relationship resulted in four offspring – three sons and a daughter, out of which the most important character to our tale is Sextus, who would later bring about the fall of the monarchy. But before that, Tarquin the proud had to ascend the throne first and to do that, he had to overthrow Servius Tullius. Soon after their marriage, Tullia encouraged her husband to usurp the throne. Tarquin the Proud took her commands to heart; he began to discredit the king, and called the Roman senators to assembly, laying out all the ways in which Servius Tullius was not fit to be the king of Rome. He disgraced Servius for being born of a slave, and for not being elected by the senate and the people. He sneered at him for having his throne handed to him by a woman, for favoring the lower classes and handing them the land that had rightfully belongs to the upper classes and for trying to break the class setup.

When Servius heard of the assembly, he raced over to where it was taking place, only to be publicly accused and disgraced by his son-in-law. Before he could really respond, Tarquinius had him thrown out bodily – down the steps of the senate house and onto the street. All of the king's supporters fled. In a daze, he tried to make his way back to the palace, but Tarquin's assassins murdered him before he could.

Meanwhile, Tullia drove her own chariot to the senate house and was the first to hail Tarquin as king.

Worried that the crowd would hurt her in a fit of chaotic violence, he bade her to return home and she reluctantly agreed. As she was returning, however, her chariot came upon the dead king's body and the driver, shocked at this sight of his monarch, stopped, unable to move. Legend has it that Tullia went into a fit of mad rage at this point – she grabbed the reins from him and drove the chariot over her father's corpse herself, spattering blood against the crude vehicle and her own clothes. The street where she disgraced him later became known as *Vicus Sceleratus,* the Street of Crime.

With that, Tarquinius and Tullia came to power as the rulers of the Roman kingdom. The people, however, were hardly pleased with them – Tarquin refused to even bury his dead father-in-law. He also killed a number of the elder Senate members, whom he suspected of still being loyal to Servius, and took to judging capital crimes without the advice of counselors. He diminished the power of the Senate over the State, and furthered his own power by betrothing his daughter to Octavius Mamilius, who was among the most elite of Latin chiefs. He launched military campaigns in quick succession – despite his victory, though, the people were extremely unhappy with his rule.

The end of Tarquin the Proud began with his foray into a war with the Rutuli. At the time, the Rutuli were a wealthy nation, and Tarquin hoped that by annexing them, he would be able to add enough to the Roman treasury to soothe the rising ire of his subjects. Meanwhile, the young noblemen fell to drinking and boasting of the virtues of their wives. Sextus, Tarquin's son, and his cousin Lucius Tarquinius Collatinus argued in earnest about their wives, and in a drunken fit, all the noblemen snuck into their homes to find out what their wives were doing. Collatinus's wife alone, Lucretia was engaged in domestic activity, and she played the part of the perfect hostess, graciously receiving the men and entertaining them. Her beauty and nobility kindled a flame in Sextus's breast, and that night, he returned to her and demanded that she give herself to him. She refused to do so, but he threatened to have her killed and claim that he had slain her when he caught her in the act of adultery with a slave.

Lucretia had no choice but to give in; wanting to protect her family from the shame of such a declaration falling upon her virtue, she submitted to him and had sex with him. However, in her mind, it was little more than rape, for as soon as he had left, she called for her husband and her father, and reported the whole affair, accusing Sextus of rape. And before anybody could talk her out of it, she pulled out a dagger and stabbed herself in the heart, killing herself while the men were still debating the truth of the story.

Lucretia's rape and her suicide triggered the end of the Roman Monarchy. Lucius Junius Brutus – who was, incidentally, another grandson of Rome's fifth king, Tarquinius Priscus – was with her husband Collatinus at the time of her death. He used it to rally the Romans to his side against Tarquin the Proud. He was the Tribune of Celeres – after the fashion instituted by Romulus centuries earlier – and as such, he was the head of the king's personal bodyguard. This meant that he had the power to call to assembly the Roman comitia, which he did. At the council, he enflamed the people against Tarquin and his wife, recounting their crimes – from the murder of Servius and their own siblings to the rape of Lucretia, each story bringing more and more of the people to his side. He also made a point to identify the class difference that Tarquin had encouraged, garnering the respect of the plebians, or the non-aristocratic commoners.

In no time at all, the Brutus persuaded the comitia to revoke the king's power and sent him to exile. Sextus, his horrific deed revealed to the people fled to the Gabii, where he wanted to avail the Roman garrison's protection. Unfortunately for him, his arrogance and misbehavior meant that he had enemies there too, and not too long after he arrived there, he was assassinated.

Beginning of the Roman Republic

The entire Roman politics underwent a complete change once monarchy was driven out of the system. Brutus called to question the idea of monarchy itself, and pointed out how the Tarquins had ruined their city, proposing that the rulers be banished. A republican form of government was introduced and accepted by all the patrician senate members Brutus had called to assembly.

According to this system, it was proposed that an interrex be appointed, who would nominate two consuls to wield the power of the king, backed by the patrician senate. An interrex would pick the prospective candidates for the consuls, and then a final vote of the curiae would accept or reject them. While the men decided to hammer out the details and fine tune this arrangement later, the temporary interim constitution was quite strong and held its own. The rationale behind the establishment of such a constitution was to ensure that there was no stagnation of power with just a selective group of people. Since the consuls and the representatives of the assemblies were elected by the people, they believed that a fiduciary relationship between the elected leaders and the citizens. People's expectations would be instrumental in driving the performance of these rulers, instead of a taste for power as the

Tarquins had displayed. This decentralization of power in an ancient civilization is completely astonishing – its effect is still seen today, where the model of the republican government followed by Ancient Romans continues to inspire many a democratic leader today.

After the death of Lucretia, and the transfer of power from the king to the State, Brutus and his party needed to acquire the assent of all the people they would henceforth be ruling. To do that, they paraded Lucretia's body through the streets, calling out for justice – Brutus even delivered a speech that moved hundreds of them to tears. A general election was quickly held to see what form of governance the plebians preferred; without question, republic won over monarchy and was instituted with Lucretia's father, Spurius Lucretius elected to be the interrex. He, in turn, nominated Brutus and Collatinus as the first two consuls, and his choice was undisputedly ratified by the curiae.

Meanwhile, the king himself, Tarquin the Proud, was at Ardea, where his wife – having fled the city in fear of the uprising – had joined him a while back. When he heard of the rebellion, he left the camp at Ardea, gathering his allies from Veii and Tarquinii; he prepared to march into Rome to win it back for himself. Brutus, as one of the consuls, was well aware of Tarquin's disposition to stay in power, and he too outfitted the Roman army to get them ready to meet their former ruler.

In a strategic move, Brutus requested that his fellow consul – Collatinius – resign from his post, since he shared his name with the hated name of Tarquinius. Stunned though he was from what he perceived as betrayal, Collatinius nevertheless agreed, and removed himself from office, with his father-in-law, the previous interrex Spurius Lucretius being selected to replace him.

Attempting to divert their attentions, Tarquin the Proud sent ambassadors to the Senate, requesting the return of all his personal property that was within the palace. His request was a trick, however, and it was soon discovered that the men were sent to subvert the leaders within the senate. All those involved with the conspiracy were put to death – including Brutus's own two sons, Titus and Tiberius, who had betrayed their father. Enraged, Brutus left Lucretius in charge of the city and marched out with the army, eager to meet the man who had claimed the lives of his family.

The legendary Battle of Silva Arsia took place, with the newly republican forces of ancient Rome fighting to defend their liberty against the deposed king, who led the Etruscan forces of Veii and Tarquinii against them. Victory went to Rome, but not without heavy loss – the first consul and the father of the Roman Republic, Lucius Junius Brutus was killed in battle.

He was succeeded by Valerius, who had him buried with great honor.

Defending the Roman Republic from Tarquin the Proud

Tarwuin the Proud was not one to be derailed easily. He wanted his throne back at any cost, and now, he turned to Lars Porsena, who ruled Clusium. The battle between Rome and Clusium led the rise of two famous Roman legends – Horatius at the bridge and Gaius Mucius Sacveola. The former is the story of how Horatius – an officer of the Roman army – held the invading army off from crossing the Pons Sublicius, which was a major bridge that that spanned the length of the Tiber River. Losing the bridge would have spelt disaster for the Romans and be defending it; Horatius saved his people, and therefore was exalted as a big hero.

Gaius Mucius Scaveola, on the other hand, is said to have brought about the end of the war itself. Accounts vary as to whether the Clusium king, Porsena, was able to occupy Rome or not – some say he did not, while others believe that he did before withdrawing his forces quickly. Either way, it was Mucius who prompted him to end the war. He was one of three hundred Roman youths who had offered to risk their own lives to assassinate Porsena, and snuck into the enemy camp. Unfortunately for him, he mistook Porsena's scribe for the king and killed him instead, and was caught very quickly after that. When he was brought before the king, however, he refused to bow down to him, instead declaring outright his intention of murder, and proclaiming himself proudly to be a loyal citizen of Rome who would defend his city with his life.

He sneered at Porsena's attempt at claiming power, and to prove to him the folly of great glory, he stuck his own hand in a sacrificial fire, without giving the slightest indication of the pain. With that, he earned himself and his descendant the name *Scaveola*, meaning 'left-handed'. Porsena, struck by his bravery, sent him back to his people, and the two warring armies. With this ended Tarquin the Proud's second attempt to demolish the Roman Republic.

But he was not Tarquin the Proud for nothing – there was no giving up until he had his throne back. The third and the last time, he approached his Latin son-in-law, Octavius Mamilius, to mount an attack on the Roman Republic. Mamilius agreed, and The Battle of Lake Regillus took place soon after, with the Roman army on one side and the Latin League on the other. Mamilius was killed in the conflict, and Tarquin the Proud had no choice but to flee the battlefield, leaving the Romans the undisputed victors. Popular legend has it that the Romans were also blessed with the divine intervention of the Gemini twins – *Castor and Pollux* – who fought for them in the guise of two young horsemen. The leader of the Roman army who led them to victory, Postumius, ordered that a temple be built in honor of the twins in the places where the army watered their horses.

Having been completely and utterly defeated, Tarquin fled Rome and later died, never returning to his city again. The Roman Republic flourished, and the system was set up properly. Governance of the city was transferred to the two consuls who were elected every year. Other than the consuls, there were other representatives of the assemblies who were elected by the people of Rome – again on a yearly basis. These consuls also held the office of commanders in chief of the Roman army. Though the idea of the establishment of a senate was to ensure that there was an equal distribution of power, the purpose was never really served. This is because most of the Senators were the former monarch rulers. There were great imbalances when it came to how the power was distributed among the citizens of Rome. It took more than a few years to get rid of these imbalances from the system. There did come a time when the representatives of the Senate were actually the voice of the citizens of Rome.

Roman Law Code

After the Republic was firmly established, in 450 B.C., a set of twelve bronze tablets was displayed in the public for their inspection. These set of tablets were later known as the twelve tables or the Roman law code. These tablets were the source of all the civil legislations that were in force in the city. It ranged from laws related to property rights to the remedies for violation of civil rights. These tablets changed the face of justice in Rome. Every citizen was aware of his rights and what were the remedies provided to him by law should his rights be affected in any way. This made it extremely difficult for the Senate to do anything against the interests of the public. In other words, these tablets ensured good governance as well. This was the polar opposite of what had transpired during the period of monarchy in Rome where the people had no knowledge of neither what the legally available rights were nor were they equipped to handle injustice.

Unfortunately, the classism that Brutus and his men sought to abolish resurfaced. As the years passed by, the Senate was filled with more and more people from powerful backgrounds. By 300 B.C., the Senate was comprised mostly of only wealthy people, mostly land-owning aristocrats, with the plebians being excluded from power once more. This was similar to how the power distribution was under monarchy. However, this Senate was much more influential than the monarch rulers.

Growth of the Republic

When the Roman republic was set up, it was regarded as the strongest empire in existence at that period of time. The empire grew exponentially, in terms of size as well as power. Sadly, though, like any other civilization, the victory streak of the Roman republic came to an end when the Gauls attacked it in the beginning of 390 B.C.

The power thirsty Gauls were on a quest to conquer more and more territory. They were famous for their prowess in battle. When the Gauls set out to expand their power beyond the Po valley, they came upon the city of Rome. Rome was regarded as a rewarding target at that point of time. When the Gallic army invaded Rome with an intention to bring it under their rule, it did more damage than the Romans anticipated. For starters, the Romans were not even expecting such an attack. Added to that was the fact that the Gallic warriors were fiercer that they had ever encountered – even the most seasoned and experienced soldiers in the Roman army were not a match to the aggressive Gallic fighters. Apart from that, the Roman army was outnumbered to a very large extent. The sole reason behind this was half the Romans had either gone into hiding or had fled the city when they heard the news of the arrival of the Gallic army at their doorsteps. Whoever stayed behind to fight knew it was a lost battle even before it began.

The Gallic army won by a huge margin and that did not come as a surprise. The Gauls celebrated their massive victory by marching through the gates of the city and looting it. They put the city under torch and brought Capitoline Hill under a siege. The siege lasted for around seven months. The Gauls agreed to put an end to the siege by leaving the city if the Romans gave them thousand pounds of gold in return for their freedom. This atrocious offer was proposed by the Gauls in an attempt to loot Rome of whatever was left of her riches one last time.

At this juncture, the ferocious leadership of Camillus strengthened the Roman army. He was instrumental in bringing about the freedom of the Romans. It is said that Camillus bought Rome's freedom with iron as opposed to the gold desired by the Gauls. With their growing strength, the Romans rose in rebellion against the Gauls and eventually succeeded in driving them out of the country. This victory was the catalyst for the many other victories that followed suit. By 264 B.C., the entire Italian peninsula came under the rule of the Romans. An ever powerful army also meant that no other conqueror was victorious in his conquest against Rome in the days to come.

Punic Wars

When the Roman Empire began growing, a new obstacle presented itself amidst the growth of the empire. Their new opponent was none other than the city of Carthage, which was reeking of prosperity.

Rome and Carthage were not meant to end up on the opposite sides of the board originally. Their relationship commenced as allies. But the thirst for more power soon saw them fighting each other from the opposite sides. Carthage was an opponent who was able to match Rome in terms of power and size. Its spread of power across the Mediterranean region made it an even more threatening opponent. In the days to come, Rome and Carthage would find themselves as a part of a series of wars. These wars were collectively referred to as the Punic wars.

First Punic War

The city of Messana was the reason behind the first Punic war. When Hiero II of Syracuse was the reason for trouble in the city, the people of Messana sought the help of the Carthaginians to fight on their behalf and restore peace in the city. Of course, Hiero II stood no chance against the mighty power of Carthage. The Carthaginians decided to use their obvious victory to their advantage and bring the city of Messana under their control. When the people of Messana sensed the power thirsty intentions of Carthage, they had no choice but to approach Rome to come to their aid. They could not think of a more worthy opponent than the Romans who would be able to expel the Carthaginians from the city.

When the Romans were approached to venture into a war against the Carthaginians, they were ready to perform the favor because of two other reasons apart from the obvious rivalry between Rome and Carthage. Messana was becoming too friendly with the cities that were being conquered by Greece at that point of time. This meant that Messana could be a serious threat to the Romans, owing to proximity reasons, should the Greeks take control over the city. The other reason was the intent to expand their empire. If Rome managed to defeat Carthage and bring Messana under its control, then it would be possible for the Romans to expand into the territory of the Sicilians. The Romans, driven by these two motives, entered into the war against the Carthaginians.

The first Punic war, which commenced in 264 B.C., lasted for twenty years. Despite their strength on land, the Romans were no match to the Carthaginians when it came to the latter's command over the sea. The naval fleet of Carthage was strong enough to give the Romans a run for their money. This war was challenging for Rome as the battle was fought both on land and in water. At the end of a long struggle that lasted for twenty years, victory was soon within the reach of the Romans. Their perseverance played an important role in their fight against Carthage. The war came to an end with a peace treaty being signed by both the cities. Unfortunately for the Romans, the treaty was not effective enough from preventing another war breaking out.

The interim period between the first and the second Punic Wars was initially relatively peace-filled, with several trade agreements set up between Rome and Carthage. When the treaty was signed, close to eight thousand of the war prisoners in Carthage were released without ransom. They also received a not inconsiderable amount of silver as war indemnity. The trouble began when there was a dispute over the peace treaty that Hamilcar Bacra of Carthage has signed with the Romans. Rome increased the indemnity that Carthage had to pay at this point, which they found difficult to do since they had liquidity issues.

To meet the required amount, however, Carthage sought help from Egypt, which at the time was a mutual ally of both Carthage as well as Rome. Unfortunately, they were unsuccessful. The result was a delay of payments to mercenary troops that had fought for Carthage in Sicily – tensions grew until the Libyan natives broke out in a rebellion, which led to the Mercenary War.

They fought against the mercenaries long and hard, and eventually won. However, they were drained out and weakened and had no choice but to accept the Roman conditions for peace, which meant that their war indemnity was increased. The tensions between Rome and Carthage fell to an extremely low point after this. War, though, did not break out until the famous Hannibal's entry into the tale.

Hannibal was Hamilcar Bacra's son. He attacked the town of Saguntum, which was under Roman protection at the time. Roman tradition holds that Hannibal had been made to swear to his father that he would never be a friend of Rome. Carthage was forbidden from crossing the river Iberus, and it was Hannibal who broke that clause, going straight on ahead to do what he was not allowed to. The Romans berated Carthage for Hannibal's actions and demanded that he be handed over to them. Carthage refused to do so and this was the straw that broke the camel's back – Rome declared war on Carthage.

Second Punic war

If you were under the impression that the first Punic war was challenging for the Romans owing to the duration, then the second Punic war that ensued would prove you wrong. What made the second Punic war even more strenuous than the first was the fact that Rome was already fighting in the First Macedonian War. This meant that the Roman army was split between these two battlefields and Rome had to enter this Second Punic war with reduced strength. Fighting two concurrent wars at the same time was not exactly conducive to winning or progressing.

This struggle witnessed the emergence of tremendous leaders on both sides, which made this war a more strategic one than the previous one. The focused leaderships of generals such as Quintus Fabius Maximus, Publius Cornelius Scipio and Marcus Claudius Marcellus guided Rome, while the aggressive brothers, Hasdrubal and Hannibal, drove Carthage.

The Second Punic war, also referred to as The Hannibalic War involved fighting in the western and eastern Mediterranean. The war to a considerable extent was initiated by Rome and not Carthage.

Hannibal led his troops with an intention to invade and capture Italy. The aggressive strategy of Hannibal was challenging enough and the Romans had to employ a handful of tactics to get him and his troops out of the way. This war lasted for around sixteen years and saw Rome emerge victorious once again. This victory not only put an end to the troubles of the miscreants, Hasdrubal and Hannibal, but also resulted in Syracuse and Hispania coming under the control of Rome.

There was a Carthaginian force present in Africa, which was the biggest trope in the whole world, with thousands of war elephants and a huge infantry. The Romans had never witnessed or fought such a huge army. Hannibal departed from Cartagena and aimed for a northwestern route, he lost a majority of his army on the way as they were reluctant to leave their homeland. He took his army through an inland route so that they could stay hidden from the Roman allies in the coastal areas. He passed through Gaul without any loss and finally met resistance at the Battle of Rhone Crossing, where a small force tried to fight against his mighty army to no avail.

At the same time, a Roman fleet was underway to invade northern Iberia. Its commanders were the brothers Cornelius Scipio and Publius Scipio, who were aware that Hannibal had left, but were surprised by the strength he left back. They sent a scouting party to look for the enemy holdfast; this small scouting party of three hundred defeated a Carthaginian force of five hundred. So, the Romans had knowledge of the enemy whereabouts and slowly marched upstream to fight them. Somehow, Hannibal evaded this force and by a hidden route reached the Alps. He also received messages from the Gallic's in Italy asking for the help of his troupe in return for helping them cross the Alps.

The first expedition of the Romans to Iberia was unsuccessful because they were not able to fight the Carthaginian troops settled there. The battle continued to northern Iberia under the leadership of Gnaeus Scipio. His brother, Publius Scipio returned to Rome because there were chances of an Italian invasion by the local tribes.

The native population of Iberia did not trust the Romans, but various encounters with them had taught them better than to revolt against their masters. Gnaeus Scipio established his base at Cissa; this area was in the middle of Hannibal's acquisitions. Hannibal left his nephew, Hanno in charge of the army situated near Cissa. Although, Hanno was easily outnumbered by the Romans, he still decided to fight against them, which led to an easy Roman victory. Hasdrubal soon made it to the battle, but was too late and had to move his troops back, but in the process he succeeded in killing a few Roman naval guards.

The Roman fleet now was a huge threat to the Carthaginians. Hasdrubal planned to destroy the fleet. His fleet had never been able to defeat the Roman fleet except one time since the First Punic war. This is why he was indecisive of fighting the Roman fleet. He moved his fleet and army together to fight off the Romans. Again, the huge Carthaginian fleet was destroyed by the Roman fleet in a battle that only lasted a day. The Carthaginians had no option but to retreat and Romans again dominated the area.

This was a very strategic position for the Romans because it prevented Carthaginians from sending reinforcements or supplies to Hannibal or to the Gauls in Italy. Hasdrubal tried to solve this problem by marching into the Roman occupied area; he was a great strategist and employed a technique to clear the field while the rest of the troops engulfed the Romans from both sides. This technique worked for some time, but then the Romans broke through the ranks and defeated the Carthaginian troops. Both the sides dealt with heavy losses and retreated back to their confined areas.

The Scipio brothers strengthened their army by hiring mercenaries; this played a key role in the war as they defeated Hasdrubal. The Romans were also successful in defeating Hannibal and stopping the Gallic uprising.

Third Punic War

As opposed to the long durations of the first two Punic wars, the third Punic war lasted only for a short span of three years. It was not so much a war as it was the spoils of the two previous battles - the Romans captured the city of Carthage and ransacked it completely. The ensuing power struggle saw the death of thousands of Carthaginians. The citizens of Carthage who survived were sold off as slaves. This war was instrumental in finally bringing Carthage under the rule of Rome.

After the second Punic war, Rome was again at war with the Hellenistic kingdoms in the east. Romans were brutal when it came to war and were suppressing the Hispanians. Carthage did not have any allies and was under a huge debt as it was forced to pay two hundred silver talents every year as indemnity.

In the Roman senate, many were in favor of destroying Carthage while others wanted to go for a more peaceful solution to the problem. For the time being the Senate agreed not to destroy Carthage.

The peace treaty that was accepted by Carthage at the end of the second Punic war was harsh and biased towards Rome. Under the treaty, any border dispute that involved Carthage was to be reviewed by the Senate who would then give permission to Carthage if they wished to. Between the third and the second Punic war, Carthage had many border disputes with the neighboring country of Numidia. In all the cases, the Senate voted in favor of Numidia since they were Roman allies.

After many years, Carthage was finally able to pay off all the debt that it owed to Rome, which meant the end of suppression by Rome and the hash peace treaty that was forced upon them. Rome did not believe this; they believed that Carthage would forever be under the control of Rome, that Carthage was subordinate to Rome and would forever comply with the peace treaty just like the Italians. Also, if the treaty was removed then Carthage was no longer obligated to pay indemnity to the Romans, which was one of the main reasons why peace had flourished between Rome and Carthage.

This was not the only reason why the Romans invaded Carthage, the Roman population was increasing every day and slowly going out of control. They needed to produce more food to feed their population. The land around Carthage was very fertile and was close to Rome, it was easily accessible and perfect for agriculture.

In 151 BC, there was another war between Carthage and Numidia. Numidia had invaded Carthaginian land and raided many small towns and villages. They soon besieged the town of Oroscopa; Carthage did not sit quietly and sent a large garrison to fight off these invaders. Carthage suffered a huge defeat at the hands of Numidia, as a result, it was forced into another huge debt that was payable to Numidia in fifty years. Rome was displeased by Carthage's action, although it was Numidia, who started the war by invading Carthaginian territory. Rome wanted Carthage to first ask for their consent before they decided to wage war against Numidia; they put up another treaty in front of Carthage that asked them to please the Roman people or there will be war.

Carthage was unsuccessful in appeasing Rome, they made several attempts, but all were futile. Rome promised Carthage that if they sent three hundred high born children as hostages, then Rome would let them keep their peace and lands. Even after this was done, Rome did not keep its promise and gathered a large army to further suppress Carthage. The army demanded that Carthage hand over every weapon, armour or ammunition that it possessed. Carthage agreed to even this, but the Romans were not satisfied. They demanded that the Carthaginians should move at least sixteen kilometers behind their boarders, while the city was to be burned. The Carthaginians were enraged by this; they mustered strength and refused to negotiate with Rome. The Romans besieged the city and this started the Third Punic War.

The Roman army landed at the allied state of Utica, there were two commanders of the army known as Manius Manillus and Lucius Marcius. They launched a strategic attack on Carthage, but were repelled by the Carthaginian army. They lost a considerable strength during the night, when the Carthaginians surprised them with a small attack. There were other soldiers who were collecting timber by the river and they were killed too. The expedition was going badly for the Romans as the Carthaginians set their fleet on fire. There was another battle at the town of Nepheris where the Romans suffered a huge defeat. After this, the Senate decided to remove Manillus from duty and replaced him with Caplurnius Piso. There was an intervention carried out by Scipio Aemilianus to save four cohorts that were trapped by the Carthaginians in a ravine. Nepheris was finally captured by the Roman army due to the brilliant and strategic attack carried out by Scipio. Piso tried to take the city of Aspis, but was unsuccessful in his attempt. Piso didn't stop here, he continued on his expedition and tried to take the town of Hippagreta, but he was again defeated and had to retreat. The Senate was unhappy with his performance in the battlefield and Scipio Aemilianus replaced him.

Carthage survived for a long time, giving the Romans a tough fight, but was still unsuccessful as Scipio Aemilianus finally defeated the army and assaulted the city. Even the citizens tried their best to fight off the invaders, but they were no match against the disciplined and vast Roman army.

Most Carthaginians had died during the war, others died due to starvation and even more died during the assault on the city. The remaining population went through many hardships. The Romans sold them into slavery and Carthage was burned down. The city was completely destroyed and soon turned into a wasteland. The remaining lands around the city were declared by Rome to be the property of the Roman Republic and added to the Roman province of Africa.

The Romans did not stop there, they embedded the city with salt to make sure that nothing could grow there and that nothing would be built there. So, even if the Punics tried to regain the city, it would be of no use.

Fall of the Empire

The subsequent wars and the strength of the Roman army were instrumental in expanding the Roman territory. The problem with Rome was that they expanded too much too fast, and did not have proper structure for governance. If an expansion of such magnitude was to survive, a solid constitution and governance systems were required. However, the constitution of Rome was not equipped to handle such a vast empire. The gap between the different sects of people grew wider as the days rolled by and this was detrimental to the expanding Roman Empire. It was not enough to have a strong army to capture a city. What was needed to sustain that control was a good government. This was precisely the reason for the crumbling of the Roman Empire.

The poor governance back home in Rome had its impact on all the other territories that were under its control. As I mentioned earlier, the Senate stopped being the representatives of the poor and became the face of the rich. In other words, Rome was tumbling back to its good old days of monarchy, which did nothing but create a huge gap between the upper class and the lower class. The poor farmers started to suffer miserably under the regime of the Senate. They were driven off their lands and denied property rights. With no land to cultivate, the farmers were drowning in poverty while the rich continued to prosper. The divide between the haves and the have-nots became a huge chasm that could not be closed.

Rome saw the emergence of social reformers such as Gaius Gracchus and Tiberius who wanted to bridge the gap between the rich and the poor and curb the inequalities. However, their efforts were futile, as they did not live to see the change they wanted to bring about. Their deaths in the hands of their enemies brought the social reforms to an end and there was no way out for the oppressed, which continued to suffer under the tyranny of the rich.

Despite its dwindling governance, there was no dearth for able leaders when it came to Rome. One such prominent leader who made things work despite the civil unrest in Rome was Gaius Marius. He was a commoner who was later elevated to the post of a consul. Owing to his reputation, he had way too many enemies and was constantly under threat. His untimely death was brought out by none other than his trusted military general, Sulla. Pompey, who succeeded Sulla, held the key to change. His military campaigns never went unnoticed. The history of Rome took a new turn under his leadership. You would agree with me on this count by the end of the next chapter.

Chapter 4: Julius Caesar

Perhaps the most famous of all Romans, Julius Caesar's reputation as a warrior and conqueror often precedes him. However, to call Julius Caesar merely a great Roman military general ruler would be a grave understatement. In all reality, the man was much more than that. He was a hugely successful statesman, general and also a famed author in Latin. He was intelligent and charismatic and he used his strengths to expand and bring the entire Roman Empire under his control. In this chapter, we shall be looking at the man himself, his rise and how he changed the face of the Roman Empire by his vision and the inevitable fall and the infamous assassination.

Julius Caesar - The Man and His Life

Gaius Julius Caesar was born into a politically influential family of that time. Both his father and mother came from families that had been rulers of provinces for many years. His father governed a province by himself whereas his mother was from a family that was extremely affluent in the political circles of the day.

He joined the army after the death of his father and needless to say, served with utmost distinction there. He quickly rose through the ranks and within a short period of time, found himself heading fleets and battalions. He returned to Rome and was duly named as the military tribune. This time was marked by the death of his Aunt and wife. His stay in Rome signaled the beginning of his political career. (This is dealt with in depth in the subsequent parts of this chapter).

As I had mentioned earlier, Julius Caesar was also a brilliant prose writer in Latin. A lot of literary works can be attributed to him but unfortunately a vast majority has been lost. Some of the most prominent and celebrated works of Julius Caesar include *"The Commentarii de Bello Gallico", "The Commentarii de Bello Civilli", "De Bello Alexandrino", "De Bello Africo"* etc. These were in essence, detailed accounts of the wars and military campaigns led by Caesar.

Rise of Julius Caesar

One of the most significant and decisive events in the political history of Ancient Rome was the formation of the First Triumvirate between Pompey, Julius Caesar and Marcus Licinius Crassus. A lot of ancillary incidences and events led to this. For instance, this alliance would not have been possible if not for the efforts taken by Caesar to reconcile Pompey and Crassus. Both of them were political rivals who wielded enormous powers individually. They had been colleagues in consulship, but they did not care for one another at all, believing that each had gone out of his way to further his own career at the expense of the other.

It was Caesar who played the binding force amongst the three when he realized the untapped potential of an alliance. Caesar and Crassus were already allies, and to further strengthen his relationship with Pompey, he even married off his daughter Julia to him. Ironically, though the triumvirate was a powerful political alliance, it lacked personal warmth or courtesy – it was simply a partnership that benefitted all three men who used it to their own ends. Pompey wanted lands for his veterans, Crassus wanted the riches and power his new position would offer him and Caesar need the backing of both the influential political figures if he wanted to accomplish anything at all. Thus, the triumvirate began to function together, though their existence was kept secret from the Senate until the Caesar's agrarian law was passed.

One of the preliminary decisions taken by this triumvirate was to decree for the redistribution of lands to the poor – Caesar's agrarian law. The trio were determined to see this through and were prepared to use force, if need be. This decision was met was met with a lot of hindrance by the opponents of the triumvirate. To counter this opposition, the alliance went no-holds-barred in their approach, case in point being the step taken by Pompey to fill the streets of Rome with armed soldiers prepared to silence the critics. Steps such as these garnered great public support for the Triumvirate.

It has to be noted that this period of Roman politics was marked by a distinct demarcation of all political sides into two basic groups, namely the "populares" and "optimates". The populares were the ones who got the vote of the public and the optimates on the other hand were the aristocrats. Due to the public support that their alliance received, Caesar was declared as the governor of three of the most prosperous provinces in Gaul.

However, the success of the triumvirate was short-lived. Crassus died in battle, defeated at the hands of the Parthians in Carrhae. This was immediately followed by the death of Julia – Pompey's wife and Caesar's daughter, who lost her life in childbirth. Caesar, the military general at heart, set out on his conquest of Gaul while Pompey seized the moment and became the consul of Rome. Caesar's invasions and conquest and the resultant power surge sowed apprehension in the mind of Pompey who joined forces with other senators. The swansong was the invasion of Italy that started the civil war in Rome. When the dust settled, Gaius Julius Caesar was left standing alone after defeating Pompey. His subsequent murder in Egypt meant that Caesar became the single ruler of Rome.

Caesar pursued Pompey to Egypt, but he arrived after the man was murdered there. Instead of returning to Rome, however, he became involved in the Egyptian Civil War between the child pharaoh and his sister, the famous Egyptian Queen Cleopatra. Caesar sided with Cleopatra, and fell for her beauty. He helped her defeat her brother after the Siege of Alexandria, and had her installed as the new ruler of Egypt. Caesar and Cleopatra never married, since Roman law only recognized marital relationships between Roman citizens. But despite the lack of labeling, their relationship flourished, and Cleopatra often visited Rome, spending time with him until his assassination, after which she formed an alliance with his second-in-command, Mark Anthony.

Caesar was appointed dictator, and he upheld his position well. He did not have his enemies murdered needlessly, instead offering pardons when he could. He won much glory on the battlefield, expanding Rome as much as he good, and focused on stabilizing the government. He had witnessed much political unrest in his time – the central government had become rather powerless, with the individual provinciaries far more influential than they should be under the governors. Instead of the constitution, it was the army that was used to achieve political goals, making political corruption a widespread phenomenon. The chasm between the rich and the poor worsened things, and though his agrarian law had been the first step to solving the problem, there was much he had yet to do.

To ensure that he would be able institute all those reforms that would stabilize Rome, Caesar went about strengthening his position in the government and slowly had the authority of other political institutions decreased. Once he was the sole dictator of the entire Empire, he began to introduce many changes within the laws – from passing a term-limit law to reduce the power of the governors to passing a family law to encourage repopulation of Italy faster.

The most important change attributed to Caesar, however, is the adoption of a new calendar. Up until then, the Roman calendar had followed the movement of the moon, which meant that their days were chaotic. Caesar instituted the Egyptian calendar instead, which was regulated by the movement of the sun, and set the length of one year to three hundred and sixty five days.

Caesar was so well loved by the masses, that the month of Quintilis was renamed July in his honor. He established a police force that protected the common people and won great victories for his people. He filed a will on the occasion of his death, naming his grandnephew, Gaius Octavius (who would later become known as Augustus Caesar), as his heir. But he did not just leave all his wealth and estate to him alone – he included a substantial gift to the people of Rome in his will, which is another reason why he was such a popular ruler.

Fall of Julius Caesar

It had to be expected that when something gains so much momentum in such a short span of time, the end would be abrupt as well. This was the case with Julius Caesar as well. He was a ruler whom the masses loved. He was one of those few leaders, who in spite of being born in an aristocratic family, was accepted and revered by the public.

But the hatred and jealousy of other senators and his enemies also grew in the same proportion as his popularity. And then took place on of the most well known events in world history - the assassination of Julius Caesar by his friend and confidante Marcus Brutus along with Gaius Cassius. Incidentally, Marcus Brutus was supposed to have been a direct descendant of Lucius Junius Brutus, the man who had fathered the Roman Republic itself.

The assassination happened as such – Mark Antony, having learned of the plot against his friend, headed off to warn him about his approaching doom. However, he was too late – the conspirators, having anticipated him, made arrangements to keep him detained until Caesar was killed.

Caesar, due to appear at a session of the Senate, arrived at the assembly, one of the conspirators, Tilius Cimber, offered him a petition to recall his exiled brother. As Caesar perused the document, the other members crowded him, 'offering their support', the hustle turned into a crowd of murderers as Casca pulled out a dagger. His killers stabbed Caesar twenty three times, and his murderers included Marcus Brutus. What is interesting is that the famous line, "*Et tu, Brute!*" may or may not have any historical backing. The line, popularized by Shakespeare's *Julius Caesar*, is no indication of Caesar's actual last words, which is a debate that scholars have been unable to resolve completely.

Still, with Caesar's assassination, there came much political chaos within Rome. Brutus and his companions marched into the city, announcing their newfound freedom from dictatorship – they were met only with silence as the common people had barricaded themselves within their homes as soon as rumors of their ruler's demise began to spread. Caesar's body lay there within the Senate room for close to three hours before any official though to remove it. Finally, he was cremated. At the place where he was cremated, the Temple of Caesar was erected, of which the altar still remains.

Aftermath of Caesar's Assassination – Disintegration of the Roman Republic

Caesar's death caused immense political upheaval within the Roman Republic. Mark Antony took over the ruling of Rome in his friend's absence, and soon after, Caesar's named heir, Octavius – called Octavian – joined forces with him, having returned to Rome upon the death of his great-uncle. Along with Marcus Aemilius Lepidus and Mark Antony, Octavian was a part of the Second Triumvirate – an alliance that would last for five years. They had a number of senators executed; their property confiscated and defeated Caesar's assassins. Both Marcus Junius Brutus and Gaius Cassius Longinus met their end at the Battle of Philippi.

The Triumvirate divided the land between themselves – Lepidus took over the ruling of Africa, Octavian remained in Italia and controlled Hispania and Gaul while Antony ruled over the eastern provinces. The relationship between Octavian and Antony, however, had begun to sour. Lepidus was soon expelled from the Triumvirate and though the remaining two maintained peace for a while, that would not last very long.

Mark Antony, already married to Octavian's sister, Octavia Minor, began an affair with Caesar's old flame – the Egyptian Queen, Cleopatra. As soon as Octavian found out, he seized the opportunity, beginning a campaign against Antony. He released to the public the truth of Antony's *Donations of Alexandria*, wherein Antony had relinquished control over much of Rome's territory to Cleopatra, and her son Caesarion. Octavian tried to convince the Senate of Antony's wrongdoings, but it was not until he married Cleopatra without first divorcing Octavia that the seed really took root.

Octavian illegally seized the will of Antony, wherein he had recognized Caesarion as Caesar's official heir, left his belongings and possessions for his children born of Cleopatra and asked to be buried with her in Alexandria and not in Rome. It was the last clause in particular which had the Senate enraged, and Octavian struck hard and fast, blaming Cleopatra for ruining Antony. As expected, the Senate voted to mount an attack on Cleopatra and Egypt, and Octavian was well aware that Antony would come to her aid, as he *did* end up doing.

The moment Mark Antony cast his lot in with Cleopatra, he was doomed – the Senate stripped him of Roman citizenship and had him labeled traitor. The war between Rome and Egypt was inevitable – on one side, Octavian brought together close to two hundred thousand Roman legionaries and on the other, Cleopatra and Antony raised a similar number, their troops a mix of both Roman and Egyptian soldiers.

The battle was long and hard, and was fought on land as well as sea. The biggest blow to Antony, though, came in the form of one of his former generals who delivered his battle strategy to Octavian. The ensuing naval battle was devastating to Antony – he had to flee, leaving his troops behind. Antony and Cleopatra were on the run now, and Octavian pursued, following them to Cyrenaica, where they approached Lucius Pinarius for help. Unfortunately for them, he had already committed to being allies with Octavian, and Antony and Cleopatra were forced to retreat to Alexandria. Octavian and Pinarius laid siege to the city, and having to watch the loss of his Roman power, Antony is said to have fallen on his sword.

Accounts vary as to what happened after. Some say he died immediately, but the most popular story is that he fell into Cleopatra's arms with an open wound on his belly. She fled with him to her mausoleum, where he died in her arms, leaving her to face Octavian by herself.

Although she also killed herself, it did not happen immediately after her lover's death. In a last ditch attempt, she opened up negotiations with Octavian, begging Caesar's grandnephew to spare her own son, who was also Caesar's heir in exchange for her own life imprisonment. Octavia, however, refused to do so, and ordered for Caesarion to be put to death, citing that two Caesars were too many. Cleopatra then died, though the cause of her death is often debated – either she died of a self-administered poisonous snakebite, or she applied a poisonous ointment to herself.

With Cleopatra dead, Rome emerged victorious. But this war had more significance that just the victory – it was the last war that the Roman Republic fought, for soon after, the Republic was dissolved and an Empire was set up once again, with Octavian as the new Emperor. And that brought to end one of the most significant and poignant chapters in Ancient Roman history.

Chapter 5: The Era of The Emperors

After the illustrious albeit tragic chapter of Julius Caesar, the Roman empire witnessed a great deal of political upheaval in the during which period, a number of rulers and emperors came on to the stage. In the course of all this, the empire continued to grow and scaled new heights.

Augustus

History had repeated itself, but with a slight twist, after the assassination of Julius Caesar. Enraged by his murder, Octavian Caesar, Mark Antony and Lepidus came together and formed the Second Triumvirate to bring about political stability, which they did, at least for a little while.

But as can be expected, there were rifts between the trio, and in the end Octavian Caesar emerged as the last standing. He went on to become the ruler of the Roman Empire under the title of Augustus. Octavian's rise to power was as smart as it was swift – he followed in the fashion of his great uncle Caesar, who was the one of the best military strategists ever to grace the Roman Empire. Octavian fashioned himself *Divi Filius* (son of god), as the adopted son of Caesar – Caesar was the first Roman figure to ever have been officially deified, with a temple to his name (Mark Antony had been appointed his *flamen,* or priest, before his death).

After defeating Cleopatra, Octavian executed the last of Mark Antony's supporters and claimed Egypt as part of his territory too. Soon after his return, the Senate members lauded Octavian with the name *Augustus,* which meant 'Exalted One'. He was smart enough to perceive a threat in the other senators and nipped it off in the bud - he stripped them off their powers! Augustus hence became the all-encompassing ruler without opposition.

He passed a series of laws that maintained the image of a Republic certainly, but left the majority of the power within the Emperor's hands. The Senate still had power and authority over territory, but the border provinces that were critical to the Empire, such as Syria, Egypt and Gaul were placed under the direct control of the Emperor and his successors.

At this point it is easy to imagine that the Roman Empire went downhill with the dissolution of the senate and the position of Augustus as the sole and supreme ruler. However the reality cannot be farther off from the truth. The rule of Augustus saw, among other things, a decline in crime and unrest, proliferation of arts and sciences, social development, and an unprecedented flourish in architecture. Literature was at its peak – poets like Horace, Ovid and Rufus wrote rich tales and even had a close relationship with Augustus himself. In fact, it was during this time that Virgil wrote *Aeneid*, which, as we saw earlier, established the Roman ancestry all the way to the Trojan War.

Strangely enough, for all that he was a dictator; Augustus managed to maintain peace within his empire. The Roman Republic had ended with the last civil war and an Empire had taken its place – Rome was now in control of the entire Mediterranean world, and after over a century of political instability, the empire would see the emergence of *Pax Romana*, or Roman Peace, sometimes called *Pax Augusta*, in honor of Augustus.

Ironically, the most difficult campaign Augustus undertook was not one of war, but of peace. The Romans, who had been continuously fighting for over two hundred years, found the sudden lull in activity strange. To them, peace was not an absence of war, but a situation when all their opponents had been beaten down, and they had to be on guard for them to arise again. Augustus now faced the problem of convincing his people to lay down arms and focus on progression and development – two terms that the Romans associated with war and gaining wealth and territory from it. But he was not a man to give up and he spent hours on a propaganda that allowed his citizens to understand the value of peace.

Under the rule of Augustus, the Roman Empire progressed like never before, it expanded its horizons and the army was mightier than ever. In short, it was indeed a golden era for the Romans in every sense.

Other Emperors after Augustus

Augustus ruled for close to fifty-six years, backed by a powerful army and devoted followers among the masses. After his death, the Senate deified him too, just like his great uncle Caesar, beginning the long tradition of deifying all popular emperors. And following in the tradition of Caesar, once again, the month of August was named after Augustus.

After the death of Augustus, many of his descendants laid claim to the throne, but as can be expected, none could match up to the excellence of Augustus himself. There are four notable cases here. The first of these men was Tiberius ruled the empire during the period 14 to 37b A.D and was despised by his countrymen. Augustus's choices for who would succeed him were limited – his nephew, Marcellus was already dead as was grandson and his friend Agrippa, who had also served as his military commander. Augustus's wife,

Livia Drusilla urged him to appoint her son from another marriage, Tiberius, as his successor and he had no choice but to agree. Tiberius took the throne in 14AD after the death of Augustus; however, he was regarded as an evil man who was rumored to have orchestrated the deaths of many of his relatives, including that of his son, Drusus Julius Caesar. He was not into political affairs – an agreement with the Senate left him retiring to Capri in 26 AD, leaving Rome initially under the rule of Sejanus (until 31 AD), and then later, Marco (until 37 AD).

Next in line came Caligula who ruled from 37 A.D to 41 A.D. Tiberius either died in 37 AD, following which the only takers to the throne was his nephew Claudius, Tiberius Gemellus his grandson and Caligula his grand-nephew. His grandson was still a child, and so Caligula was chosen to rule. For the first half of his reign, he was heralded as a good ruler; by the time his rule drew to a close, he was considered a tyrant and an incestuous murderer. He ruled only for four years – in 41 AD, as he was murdered by the Praetorian Guard.

After him came Emperor Claudius for the period ranging from 41 A.D to 54 A.D. He was not authoritarian as his predecessors had been; his only significant contribution to the pages of history was spearheading the successful invasion of Britain. His reign ended when his wife, Agrippina the Younger, poisoned him in 54 AD.

The next and last emperor of this dynasty was Nero. He was Agrippina's son from a former marriage, who took the throne, since Claudius's own son Britannicus had not reached manhood when his father died. Nero was a completely incapable ruler who unceremoniously put an end to the line of Augustus's dynasty by committing suicide. He is widely known to the populace as the first persecutor of Christians. He was also suspected of starting the Great Fire of Rome, which was a fire, started in the night of the 18th and the 19th of July in 64 AD. It lead to devastation and destroyed more than half the city and ran its course for over six days before finally being put out. While many credit Nero for having provided prompt relief measures, still more accuse him of being the organizer in the first place. Nero himself blamed the fire on the Christians, and continued to prosecute them – a practice that continued until the emergence of Constantine.

Nero faced a number of revolts during his reign, and although he defeated many of those rebels, he was unable to win against the soldiers led by Servius Sulpicius Galba, who drove him from the throne. The Senate then declared him a public enemy, and faced with an execution, he chose to kill himself, ending the *Julio-Claudian Dynasty* that began with Augustus.

His reign was one of tyranny and extravagance – not only did he cause Christians endless misery, he executed his own mother and is also rumored to have murdered his younger stepbrother, Britannicus by poison.

The most significant ruler to occupy the throne of Rome after Nero was Vespasian, who established the *Flavian dynasty*. After Nero's suicide in 68 AD, there was a year of civil war within the Empire – the first since Mark Antony's death more than two centuries earlier in 30 BC. Within the span of a year, Rome saw the rise and fall of four kings – Galba (who had defeated Nero), Otho, Vitellius and Vespasian. Not surprisingly, this interim year was known as the *Year of the Four Emperors*.

Vespasian's rule was between 69 A.D and 79 A.D. He had been a general under Nero and Claudius, and had fought in the First Jewish-Roman War that the former had instituted. The most notable contribution by this emperor was the construction of the Flavian Amphitheater, today known as the *Colosseum*. With Vespasian, the Flavian Dynasty was established. The most important decision taken by the Flavian rulers was to restore the powers of the senate.

His sons, Titus and Domitian, followed him. The former had a very short rule, lasting only three years, from 79-81 AD. He completed the Amphitheater begun by his father, only to die of fever in 81 AD, when his brother Domitian succeeded him. The period of Titus was also marked by a natural catastrophe of unprecedented magnitude - the eruption of Mount Vesuvius volcano. Titus played a commendable role in restoring life to normalcy in the aftermath of the large-scale destruction spewed by the volcanic eruption that witnessed complete obliteration of the cities of Pompeii and Herculaneum. Domitian, on the other hand, was a rather unpopular ruler. He assumed totalitarian rule, and fashioned himself a god among his people, often referring to himself as *Dominus et Deus*, or Master and God. The nobles did not enjoy his kingship, and he was murdered in 96 AD.

After Domitian, the last of the Flavian rulers, the senate appointed Nerva as the ruler for the period 96 A.D to 98 A.D. The reign of Nerva heralded another era of prosperity for the Roman Empire. Nerva was the first to be chosen emperor since Octavian had been honored with the title of Emperor. He had served as an advisor to Nero; now, as emperor, he restored much of prosperity Domitian's rule had taken away.

Nerva's rule began the last golden age of Rome. There is a major reason for this. All the four emperors who came after Nerva, namely Trajan (98 A.D to 117 A.D), Hadrian (117 A.D to 138 A.D), Antonius Pius (138 A.D to 161 A.D) and Marcus Aurelius (161 A.D to 180 A.D) were rulers not by hereditary succession. Instead, they were named by the outgoing ruler based on their merit and capability. Together with Nerva, the five kings were named as the *Five Good Emperors*.

All four of Nerva's successors made their own contribution to the prosperity of the Roman Empire. Trajan freed many who had been unjustly imprisoned by Domitian, and returned much of the property the tyrannical emperor had confiscated. He also successfully won wars against Dacia and Parthia and thereby expanded the boundaries of the empire. Hadrian on the other hand – nominated by Trajan before he died of edema in 117 AD – was interested more in the betterment of the empire from within and bought along many reforms to this effect. He avoided wars, and focused on construction, building fortifications and walls. The famous Hadrian's Wall between Roman Britain and Scotland was, as the name suggests, built during this time. As a lover of culture, he promoted it, particularly the Greek culture, for which he held the highest regard. He forbade torture and traveled nearly daily among his provinces to identify the state of his people through his own eyes.

Hadrian died in 138 AD and was succeed by Antonius Pius, who maintained the peace that was prevalent in the empire when he took over. He made few notable changes within his governance. The most important contribution he made to the Roman Empire was the expansion of Roman Britain by invading southern Scotland. He also built the Antonine Wall, and carried Hadrian's policy of humanizing laws forward.

However, the peace was short-lived once Marcus Aurelius took charge after Antonius's death in 161 AD. He waged costly wars against Parthia and Armenia. On top of that the empire was continuously under the threat of invasion by Germanic tribes from the North. The rule of Marcus Aurelius broke another tradition when he disregarded the procedure for selection of the next ruler based on merit. Instead he proclaimed his son Commodus as the next ruler of Rome, whose rule was the beginning of the Roman decadence.

Chapter 6: Disintegration Of The Roman Empire

The once glorious Roman Empire did meet its end eventually. In this chapter, let us look at how the mighty empire soon disintegrated into nothing.

Decline of the Roman Empire

When Commodus became the king in 180 A.D., the decline of the Roman Empire started becoming a reality. Even though his reign was for a brief period of twelve years, it was enough to cause sufficient damage. He took part in gladiatorial combats regularly, which were widely known for their brutality, and killed many Roman citizens without thought. His decisions disappointed not just the public but also his ministers. Unsurprisingly, this resulted in his death in the hands of his own cabinet of ministers. Commodus's death resulted in the eruption of another civil war in Rome, and the year following his demise is called as the *Year of the Five Emperors*. As the name suggests, five kings – Clodius Albinus, Pertinax, Pescennius Niger, Didius Julianus, and Septimius Severus – rose and fell, before Septimius established himself emperor. He and his successors governed with the legions' backing. Unfortunately, they had to pay for this backing with money, which proved to be one of the main causes for the financial crisis that marked the *Crisis of the Third Century.*

Many emperors assumed the throne in the years to come but they were not able to revive the past glory of Rome. What worsened the situation was the disintegration of Rome into four parts. Rome was divided into four for easy governance and for the restoration of peace within the city. However, this did not have the desired result in terms of stability.

Diocletian, hailed as the Imperator, was the one to introduce this form of government, known as the Tetrarchy. The Empire was split into four and left under the rule of four emperors. The first was under Diocletian in the east; the second under Maximian in the west. Galerius in the east and Flavius Constantius in the west ruled under them, bringing the total number of segments up to four.

Diocletian rid Syria of the Persians who plundered the country and fought off barbarian tribes as well. He adopted a number of Eastern monarchs' behaviors, including having anyone in the emperor's presence prostrate himself. Perhaps the most significant aspect of Diocletian's rule is that he did not use a disguised form of Republic, like all his predecessors since Augustus had done. He was an emperor and he proclaimed his status proudly.

Diocletian was an avid persecutor of the Christians. The tradition, begun with Nero, continued with Diocletian, who ordered the destruction of all Christian churches and forbade worship of Christ. Ironically, he was the first Roman emperor to resign, abdicating in 305 AD with Maximian.

When Constantine assumed the throne in 324 A.D., Rome was united into a single entity once again. This unification was instrumental in bringing about internal peace. Constantine himself had converted to Christianity and as such, he issued the *Edict of Milan*, which granted liberty for the Christians to practice their faith. Under the reign of Constantine, Christianity was declared as the official religion of Rome. With him, the Christianization of the Empire, and then, Europe begun – a practice later carried forward by the Catholic Church in the Middle Ages.

To celebrate his own victory and the importance of his religion – Christianity – he had the city of Byzantium rebuilt. He dubbed it Nova Roma, or the *New Rome,* and declared it to be the new capital of the empire. The city soon gained another moniker – Constantinople, or *City of Constantine*. To be honest, Rome's significance as the capital was long diminished; after the Crisis of the Third Century, Mediolanum was appointed capital initially, followed by Ravenna. After that, different members of the Tetrach established half a dozen new capitals; so having Byzantium made the new one was no new thing.

The peace that was restored by the unification was not a long lasting one. The death of Constantine saw the division of Rome into two parts. The last of the Constantinians led Rome into battle against Persians and Germanic barbarians, but they lost, soon after which Rome fractured into two factions - the Western and the Eastern Empires. The Eastern Roman Empire was ruled by Arcadius and the Western by Honorius, both of whom were brothers.

In 408, a general named Stilicho tried his best to reunite the two factions in an attempt to repel a barbarian invasion. However, he was unsuccessful and the empire further fractured, with no hope of coming back together again. The fifth century watched as the Western fraction of the Empire lost a significant amount of territory lost, beginning with the Vandals conquering North Africa. Gaul was lost to the Visigoths and Hispania to the Suebi. The central government under pressure abandoned Britain. To make matters worse, Attila the Hun constantly attacked the Empire, leaving them weak and vulnerable. The once celebrated provinces of the Roman Empire were passed off to other rulers one by one.

The end of the Roman Empire came with the plunge of the world and history into the Middle Ages. General Orestes refused to comply with the demands of the barbarian allies who were now a major part of the Roman army. He rebelled against them, trying to evict them from Italy, but was defeated instead. The tribes invaded Reavnna and Odovacar, the Germanic prince, killed Orestes's son, Romulus Augustus in 476 AD, and officially, historians prescribe this event to mark the end of the Ancient World as wheels of time turned to usher in the Middle Ages.

On the other hand, the Eastern Empire fared differently. It would survive for close to thousand years after the fall of its Western counterpart by becoming the most stable Christian institution during the Middle Ages. However, the fall of the Eastern Empire did happen much later. They survived and emerged victorious against the Islamic expansions. They warred against Arabs factions that captured southern Italy and Sicily and reclaimed their land.

In 1000 AD, the Eastern Empire was still flourishing and thriving. But its end was nigh; they were defeated in the *Battle of Manzikert*. The aftermath of this war proved disastrous; it sent the empire into a negative tailspin. The empire saw two full decades of internal strife and their situation was not helped when Turkic invasions began, paving the way for Emperor Alexius

I Commenus to call to the Western European kingdoms for help.

What he could not have expected was the response of the West, which instituted the Crusades. The Sack of Constantinople by the participants in the Fourth Crusade took place and this conquest of the capital of the Empire fractured what was left of it into smaller, successor states. Imperial forces managed to bring Constantinople back under their control, but by that time, the Roman Empire had shrunk in size – it had become miniscule compared to what it had once been. The last of the Byzantine Empire collapsed without much protest when Mehmed II took Constantinople on the 29th of May 1453.

Roman Religion

The Roman religion was centered on the ethnic and ancient religion followed by the people of Rome. It also included the religious practices that were brought in by different territories captured by Rome. The Romans were extremely religious; there wasn't any important task that they carried out without consulting their gods. They believed that the reason for their success in wars and as a city was due to their devotion towards their gods, who helped them against all foes. Rome's religion can be traced to its founder, who promoted the worship of divine deities among the population. Rome had many kings who had relations directly with the gods, such as the Sabine king Nuna Pompilius, who wrote many books on how to perform rites to appease the gods. Rome's religion is central to its identity as a great nation.

In ancient Rome, the church and the state were not separate. Many times people who held important political offices also acted as augurs or pontiffs. Priesthood wasn't something sacred with specific rules; priests were allowed to have families and children.

Every Roman household prayed to the gods, religion was incorporated into their daily lives. It was necessary for every house to have a shrine where the family could pray and perform rituals. Springs and groves were considered as auspicious places to pray to the gods and many visited them daily. Even the Roman calendar was centered on religious dates; it mentioned specific dates dedicated to the worship of deities. Women mostly carried out religious practices and they formed a major part of Rome's famous priesthood, known as the Vestals.

Romans worshiped a great number of deities; most of their deities were influenced by Greek culture, since their ancestors were Greek. They found common ground among their religion and Greek myths, to form their religious practices.

Jupiter

In Roman mythology, Jupiter is the king of gods and the God of lightning and the sky. Jupiter was the most closely related to the Romans and the most worshipped deity till Christianity became dominant in the empire. Romans asked for his blessing before they went to war, believing that they will only succeed if they please Jupiter. Jupiter's Greek equivalent in Zeus, the Romans accepted him as their god during the transition of Greek culture into Roman. In mythology, he had direct relations with Numa Pompilius the second king of Rome; he taught him various rituals and sacrifices that have to be made to please the gods. So, in reality it was Jupiter, who helped the Romans in establishing their religious practices.

Jupiter originated from the sky with the eagle as his symbol, and a thunderbolt as his weapon. His symbol, the eagle has influenced a lot of Roman relics, such as the sign of the Roman army and the coinage system of Rome had the picture of an eagle minted on it. During auspices, the eagle had precedence over other birds and was a good omen. He has been depicted in art as an eagle holding a thunderbolt in its talons. Since, he is the god of sky, he's omnipresent, because of which he was a divine witness to every deed done by man. Every time someone took an oath, they did it in his presence, which became the symbol of justice, liberty and proper governance.

He had many children, namely Mars, Vulcan, Minerva and Hercules. He was married to Juno and his siblings were Neptune and Pluto. In Greek mythology, he was the son of Saturn, the evil Titan who ate his own children when he heard the prophecy about his children overthrowing him and becoming gods.

The Romans believed themselves to be sacred and superior to any other nation because they had worshipped Jupiter the longest and had his favor. Every important office in Rome, its internal organization and foreign relations were the embodiment of Jupiter's trait of justice and good governance. His image was the representation of Rome, the Republican and Imperial Capitol were his symbol of power and influence. All the consuls, even the king swore an oath to Jupiter before they started presiding over their respective office. The Romans thanked him by sacrificing a white ox, with gilded horns in his name.

Juno

Juno is the Roman goddess of marriage and the queen of the gods. She is the daughter of Saturn, and a sibling to Jupiter, Neptune and Pluto. She earned her status as the queen due to her marriage with Jupiter. She's also the mother of Mars and Vulcan. Juno's main role was as a goddess for women. She took care of the women of Rome and helped them through childbirth. She took care of their children as well till they were of age and praying to her on the day of the marriage was a famous ritual as she was also the goddess of marriage. Her Greek equivalent was known as Hera. She was the special consular to the Roman Empire, and its patron goddess, she was known as Regina. Jupiter, Minerva and Hera together were worshipped as the triad on the Capitol.

Although in Greek mythology she wasn't a warlike goddess, this aspect adorned to her in the Roman religion. She was depicted with a peacock, wearing a goatskin cloak and armed with knives.

She had many connections with vitality, zest and energy. She could also grant eternal youthfulness if she was pleased with someone's devotion. She is the protector of the realm and depicts divine sovereignty.

Neptune

Neptune was the Roman god of water, specifically the sea. He is the brother of Jupiter and Pluto and his Greek equivalent is Poseidon. Jupiter, Pluto and Neptune together presided over the three realms of the world, the sky, the underworld and the water. Salacia was his paramour.

He was also worshipped by the Romans as the God of Horses. He and Minerva once had a competition to be the patron of Rome, but he could not impress the Romans while Minerva provided them with knowledge, which made the Romans picked her as the Patron Goddess.

The Romans have always had a conflicted relationship with Neptune, since they lived inland; at first they denied the existence of a God of Sea. Till the start of the Roman Empire, they didn't even have ships or fleet to voyage on the ocean, till they were forced to do so in the Punic war. Although, they never had the blessings of Neptune when it came to sea voyages, they still succeeded in destroying the Carthaginian fleets. There was only one temple dedicated to Neptune in all of Rome near Circus Flaminius.

Romans did pray to him occasionally, by sacrificing bulls, he's the only God except Apollo and Mars to whom sacrificing bulls is a good omen.

Pluto

Pluto was the god and ruler of the underworld in Roman mythology. His Greek equivalent was Hades, he was sometimes also called by this name in Rome and the underworld was also known as Hades in some places. In Roman mythology Pluto was less sinister and negative than he was in Greek mythology, which is why he was never worshipped in Greek and was cast out of Mount Olympus. Pluto did have temples in Rome, where he was seen as the god that helps the dead find peace and quiet. He was also the god of wealth because rare and rich materials were found underground, so he had full control over them. He was a very strict ruler, he emphasized on organizing the underworld, but was a very caring husband to Persephone. Hades on the other hand kidnapped Persephone and forced her into a marriage.

Pluto was siblings with Jupiter and Neptune. There was a three way division of the rule amongst them and Pluto got the underworld while Jupiter got the sky and Neptune the water. He's always had a budding rivalry with his brothers since he was cast out by them and left to control the least important realm. His major role in mythology was the abduction of Persephone and his narrative with various heroes of the old age whom he helped or killed, such as Orpheus.

Apollo

Apollo is the Roman and Greek god of music, poetry, art, oracles, archery, plagues, medicine, sun, light and knowledge. He was considered to be the ideal athletic youth; he is the son of Zeus and Leto. He has a twin sister known as Artemis, who was a huntress and also a skilled archer. She handled the opposite duties of Apollo, such as being the goddess of the moon.

He was the patron god of Delphi; he was also the god who blessed the Oracle of Delphi with her powers. He's also the god who healed people and created medicines to save them while at the same time his anger brought plagues and ill-health. He's also seen as a shepherd who tends to his flock and his favorite musical instrument is the Iyre, created for him by Hermes. Once, when Apollo was just a kid, Hermes stole his sheep which enraged Apollo a lot. Apollo wanted to punish Hermes but stopped, when Hermes gave him the Iyre as an apology.

He's also confused with Helios, the god of sun and similarly his sister is confused with Selene, the goddess of the moon.

Hera was jealous when she discovered that Leto was pregnant with Zeus's son, so she banished her from giving birth on land. Leto found an island that was on water, known as Delos, here she gave birth to Apollo and Artemis, and promised to the people of Delos that her children would be favorable towards the island. The people of the island accepted her and this island became sacred to Apollo.

Hera even went ahead to stop Leto by abducting the goddess of childbirth known as Eileithyia. The other gods wanted to help Leto so they tricked Hera by giving her a long amber necklace; she was so fascinated by it that she forgot all about Eileithyia. Artemis was born before Apollo and then she helped her mother in giving birth to her brother.

Soon after his birth Apollo saved his mother from the dragon Python, who lived in Delphi. Hera had sent him to kill Leto, Apollo asked Vulcan to give him a bow and arrow to protect his mother. He killed the snake with a bow, but was punished for this since Python was the son of Gaia.

Hera then sent the giant Tityos to rape Leto. This time Artemis and Apollo fought together to kill Tityos. Zeus helped his two children by throwing Tityos into Tartarus. He was tied to the floor and a vulture ate his liver every day.

Mars

Mars was the Roman god of War and also the

guardian of farmers. He was the second most important deity of Rome and was worshipped by many. He was the major god to whom the Romans prayed before they went to war. There were many festivals dedicated to him, most of them were held in March, as the month was named after him and in October, which was the month of harvest and military campaigning.

His Greek equivalent is Ares, but fundamentally both the gods differ a lot. Ares was a god who favored violence and nothing else while Mars was a god that favored military discipline and honor. Jupiter, Mars and Quirinus formed the Archaic Triad. Ares was a destructive force while Mars represented power through war and military conquest.

Mars was also the protector of Rome and had temples outside Rome, but later on, there were a few temples that were made in his name inside the Roman boundaries. He also had a famous love affair with Venus.

Ares was the son of Zeus and Hera, but Mars was different, he was the son of Juno alone. Juno did not appreciate that Jupiter had created Minerva from his head without consorting with her. So, she asked the goddess Flora for help in giving birth alone. Flora searched the world for a magical flower, used it to impregnate Juno by putting it on her belly. Juno went away to a secluded island to give birth to Mars.

Mars had many consorts such as Venus, Nerio and Silvia. His symbol is a shield with a spear. He is the brother of Hercules, Minerva, Vulcan and Bellona. His sacred animals include the woodpecker, wolf and bear.

The various temples dedicated to him all had an altar known as the Altar of Mars to sacrifice animals that please him such as a pig, ram and bull.

Venus

Venus is the Roman goddess of love, beauty and desire. She was considered to be the mother of the Romans through her son Aeneas; he fled Troy and was responsible for the formation of Rome. Even Julius Caesar accepted her as his ancestor. There were many cults dedicated to her worship and there were many religious festivals where she was worshipped.

Her Greek equivalent is Aphrodite and she is one of the most famous goddesses in the west as the patron of beauty and love.

Venus had various signs and symbols that were similar to Aphrodite such as roses and myrtle. Venus was married to Vulcan, but still had an affair with Mars; she also had a son with Mars known as Cupid.

There were many temples dedicated to Venus in Rome.

Mercury

Mercury is a major Roman god of financial gain, commerce and poetry. He is one of the Dil Consentes of ancient Rome. He is also famous as the god of trickery and guiding souls to the underworld. He is the son of Jupiter and Maia, he acts as a messenger of the gods too, and he connects the mortal and immortal world by passing messages. His Greek form is known as Hermes. In old mythology, Mercury was supposed to send the nymph Larunda to underworld by guiding her but he fell in love with her on the way and made love with her. She became pregnant with his children and gave birth to the Lares, also known as the invisible household gods.

Mercury has influenced the Roman culture in many ways, the planet Mercury was named after him and also the liquid element. He wasn't prayed to much by the Romans because he was not one of the earliest deities but he did have a few temples and his own festival on May 15, known as Mercuralia. It was a sacred festival for merchants who threw water on their heads from a well at Porta Capena. They believed that this would get them the favor of Hermes.

Minerva

Minerva was the Roman goddess of trade, strategy, intelligence and knowledge. She is the daughter of Jupiter alone and was born from his head with weapons. Jupiter heard a prophecy, according to which his own child would overthrow him. So, after he made love to the Titaness Metis, he realized his mistake and ate Metis whole to make sure that she could not give birth and he would always be the god of sky. While Metis was inside Zeus, she made various weapons for her child so he/she could protect himself/herself. The constant ringing and hammering gave Jupiter a headache. Jupiter asked for Vulcan's help to relieve him from the pain, Vulcan made a device to split Jupiter's head and from it emerged Minerva with the weapons and armour her mother had forged.

Her Greek equivalent is Athena and she never had any sexual relations. She was the virgin goddess of weaving, music, poetry, wisdom and magic. Her symbol is an owl; she is often depicted in art with it.

Tinia, Uni and Minerva together formed the holy triad. She was also part of the Capitol triad with

Jupiter and Juno. All the healers in Rome worshipped her because she was the goddess of doctors and medicine. She also became the goddess of war as Romans prayed to her for strategic help.

Vulcan

Vulcan was the Roman god of fire; he had supreme control of volcanoes and is also the god of metalwork and forge. His symbol is a hammer as he was a blacksmith who worked to create brilliant relics. There was a specific festival dedicated to him in ancient Rome known as Vulcanalia that was held on 23 August. His Greek equivalent is Hephaestus, the god of smiths.

Vulcan was a major god in Rome; he had a shrine dedicated to him at the foot of the Capitoline known as Vulcanal, it was built by the ancient king of Rome, Titus Tatius. Earlier the Romans believed that a temple dedicated to Vulcan should be built outside the boundary of the city but later on as the city expanded it came inside the boundary of the city. On 23 August, the Vulcanalia was celebrated at his temple, with various sacrifices made to appease him. He had another temple dedicated to him known as Campus Martius.

Since Vulcan was equivalent to his Greek form Hephaestus, he was associated with metalwork and forging. Many Roman relics that were found later on had his depiction on them which showed that the Romans used his imagery to bless their creations. Hephaestus was related to both the constructive and destructive use of fire while Vulcan was only related to the constructive nature of fire.

Janus

Janus was the Roman god of transition, beginnings and ending. Hence, he was the god of doors, paths and choices. He is depicted with two faces in Roman arts because he is the god of choices, his two aspects have different natures and offer different choices. It also shows that he looked at both the past and the future. It is believed that January was named after him but it is disputed whether it was him or Juno.

A temple was built to his name by Numa Pompilius, since he is the god of beginnings and endings; the doors to his temples were opened to depict the start of a war and closed when the war ended. He also had functions related to birth, travel and harbors.

There were no specific rites to praise Janus but rather the king himself used to sacrifice in his name, after the monarchy was ended; the King of the Sacred Rites did this. It was necessary for priests to worship and invoke Janus during any religious ceremony. This meant that at the beginning of every festival or prayers to any god, Janus was prayed to first.

Janus had no Greek equivalent and is said to only exist in Roman mythology but some scholars say that he was present in Greek mythology by the same name.

Conclusion

Civilizations rise and fall, but few of them have had the long-lasting glory and power of the Ancient Romans. Unfortunately, no empire is going to last forever, and they were no exception to the rule. Like any other great kingdom that fell, Ancient Rome too, had to give in to the passage of time.

No civilization was free from errors of governance. History has seen many glorious empires coming to an end because of various reasons. While some hit rock bottom because of wrong military decisions, the others were the victims of poor governance. As you might have figured out by now, the lack of a sound constitution and consistent leadership were the important reasons behind the fall of the Empire.

Having enjoyed more than a millennium as independent people, the Ancient Romans lost their home and history to not only the ravages of time, but poor governance and much in fighting. Historians attribute Rome's fall to the loss of its Republicanism, military tyranny, Rome's endless obsession with war and conquering, economic stagnation, classism and the like. A number of pagans have argued that Christianity and the decline of the traditional Roman religion of paganism were to be blamed for the loss of the Empire. These were supported by a number of modern rationalist philosophers, who believed that this change from a martial religion to a more pacifist type of worship meant that the number of good soldiers in the army was reduced. To oppose them, many Christians (including Saint Augustine) countered the sinful nature of Ancient Roman society itself brought about their downfall.

Whatever the reason for its defeat, in the ebb and flow of time, the great Roman civilization was wiped away. There is no doubt that Rome did have some great leaders. However, the issue lay in the fact that these great leaders were great soldiers as opposed to great politicians. Their aggressiveness coupled with their thirst for power helped Rome expand its Empire. But their shortcomings in terms of governance made it difficult for the Roman Empire to survive. What is ironic is that the Roman Republic was the first of its kind; it expressed tenets of liberty and independence that continues to inspire governments of today, millennia after it was instituted. In the end, though, man had no choice but to give in to the inevitable and the curtains fell on the play of the Ancient Roman Empire that had lasted for more than a millennium and had seen close to seven hundred years as the one of the greatest powers in human history.

I hope you found this book an informative and exciting read!

If you enjoyed this journey you may be interested in my other books.

Greek Mythology: Guide to Ancient Greece, Titans, Greek Gods, Zeus and More!

Hyperurl.co/greekmyth

Alexander: The Great Leader and Hero of Macedonia and Ancient Greece

hyperurl.co/alexthegreat

Egypt: Egyptian Mythology and the Secrets of the Gods

Hyperurl.co/egypt

Greek Mythology: Myths and Legends of the Gods, Titans, Zeus, Olympians and More!

Hyperurl.co/greekmyths

Viking Mythology: Ancient Myths, Gods and Warriors

Hyperurl.co/Viking

GREEK GODS: Myths, Legends and Ancient History

hyperurl.co/greekgods

Printed in Great Britain
by Amazon